HTA + VBSCRIPT

+

MICROSOFT.ACE. OLEDB.15.0 = YOU CODE SMARTER AND FASTER

*Please Judge this book by it's cover.
The program is inside*

Richard Edwards

STOP WISHING FOR IT

It is right here

Looking for something you or a friend of yours could use to charge up your new year with a program that works to produce results. Here it is!

This one uses Microsoft.ACE.OleDb.15.0 and the code to make it is in this book. So, what does it do?

Well, for one thing you can open all older versions of Access databases with the extension of .mdb. But they had to be created between 1998 and 2007. Otherwise, you will get an error telling you that the database was created by a newer version of Access.

Purchase the version of this product – past that time – that is in sync with the provider requirements. I have one for each version of the ACE.OLEDB provider up to Microsoft.ACE.OLEDB.15.0.

When you click the first Go button at the very top and right of the program, brings up a common dialog box:

Which I used to connect to an older database file: NWind.mdb.

Once I have done this, I click the other go button which lists all the tables and views and automates the process of creating creatable queries as seen below:

Once I decide which Query to run, because the table type, orientation and control type are set to table, Multi-Line Horizontal and span, respectively html code is generated:

The Code

```
<html>
<head>
<title>Products</title>
<style type='text/css'>
body
{
     PADDING-RIGHT: 0px;
     PADDING-LEFT: 0px;
     PADDING-BOTTOM: 0px;
     MARGIN: 0px;
     COLOR: #333;
     PADDING-TOP: 0px;
     FONT-FAMILY: verdana, arial, helvetica, sans-serif;
}
table
{
     BORDER-RIGHT: #999999 3px solid;
     PADDING-RIGHT: 6px;
     PADDING-LEFT: 6px;
     FONT-WEIGHT: Bold;
     FONT-SIZE: 14px;
     PADDING-BOTTOM: 6px;
     COLOR: Peru;
     LINE-HEIGHT: 14px;
     PADDING-TOP: 6px;
     BORDER-BOTTOM: #999 1px solid;
     BACKGROUND-COLOR: #eeeeee;
     FONT-FAMILY: verdana, arial, helvetica, sans-serif;
     FONT-SIZE: 12px;
}
th
```

This is what the code looks like inside the program. Of course, it is a lot clearer in the program than the image shows. At this point, clicking on View Results on the left side of the screen:

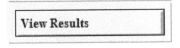

Will show you this:

ProductID	ProductName	SupplierID	CategoryID	QuantityPerUnit
1	Chai	1	1	10 boxes x 20 bags
2	Chang	1	1	24 - 12 oz bottles
3	Aniseed Syrup	1	2	12 - 550 ml bottles
4	Chef Anton	2	2	48 - 6 oz jars
5	Chef Anton	2	2	36 boxes
6	Grandma	3	2	12 - 8 oz jars
7	Uncle Bob	3	7	12 - 1 lb pkgs.
8	Northwoods Cranberry Sauce	3	2	12 - 12 oz jars
9	Mishi Kobe Niku	4	6	18 - 500 g pkgs.
10	Ikura	4	8	12 - 200 ml jars
11	Queso Cabrales	5	4	1 kg pkg.
12	Queso Manchego La Pastora	5	4	10 - 500 g pkgs.

Of course, how flashy it looks will depend on the stylesheet that you use and the additional tag that you partnered with it.

What is being offered

There is no such thing as a bugless program. Glitches happen. However, the routines – for static, dynamic, cloaked and bound have been tested and work. Additionally, the HTML ADO Coding option, pictured below, only works with the Bound coding option.

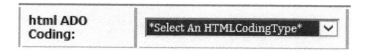

You have four basic formats:

Binding Types:	Static	☑	Dynamic	☐	Cloaked	☐	Bound	☐

Each one of these formats allows you to mix Table types: Report or table; Orientation: Multi-Line Horizontal, Multi-Line Vertical, Single-Line Horizontal and Single Line vertical; Additional Tags: Button, Combobox, Div, Listbox, Span, Textarea and Textbox; and 10 style sheets.

Meaning you have 560 ways to create Static, Dynamic, Cloaked or Bound outputs and that there are 2,240 ways you can produce html code from one database and one table.

If each only averaged 30 lines of code, those 2.240 ways to produce code would be the same outcome as one programmer could create in a year. The Products table using the Shadow Box stylesheet, came out to 1,114 lines and that took about 30 seconds to produce and display. And that is from the time the program started up to the time the view the results button was clicked on.

This program can list all the providers, drivers and ISAMS that are installed on the machine the program is running on, too.

The e-mail program is designed to be used with your Gmail account. If you don't have one, well, its probably not something you'd get any warm and fuzzies from.

If you do, the newer version of Gmail, has a switch that must be enabled in order to use it.

THE CODE NEEDED TO MAKE THIS PROGRAM WORK FOR YOU

From below the line is the code you need to create this program:

```
<html xmlns:v="urn:schemas-microsoft-com:vml">
<HEAD>
<HTA:Application
    ID = "Excalibur"
    APPLICATIONNAME = "Excalibur"
    Scroll = "no"
    SINGLEINSTANCE = "No"
    WORKSTATE = "Normal"
>
<head>
<title>Excalibur</title>
<style type='text/css'>
v\:*{ behavior: url(#default#VML);}
body
{
    PADDING-RIGHT: 0px;
    PADDING-LEFT: 0px;
    PADDING-BOTTOM: 0px;
    MARGIN: 0px;
    COLOR: #333;
```

```
    PADDING-TOP: 0px;
    FONT-FAMILY: verdana, arial, helvetica, sans-serif;
}
Table
{
    BORDER-RIGHT: #999999 1px solid;
    PADDING-RIGHT: 1px;
    PADDING-LEFT: 1px;
    PADDING-BOTTOM: 1px;
    LINE-HEIGHT: 8px;
    PADDING-TOP: 1px;
    BORDER-BOTTOM: #999 1px solid;
    BACKGROUND-COLOR: #eeeeee;
    filter:progid:DXImageTransform.Microsoft.Shadow(color='silver',
Direction=135, Strength=16)
}
th
{
    BORDER-RIGHT: #999999 3px solid;
    PADDING-RIGHT: 6px;
    PADDING-LEFT: 6px;
    FONT-WEIGHT: Bold;
    FONT-SIZE: 14px;
    PADDING-BOTTOM: 6px;
    COLOR: darkred;
    LINE-HEIGHT: 14px;
    PADDING-TOP: 6px;
    BORDER-BOTTOM: #999 1px solid;
    BACKGROUND-COLOR: #eeeeee;
    FONT-FAMILY: font-family: Cambria, serif;
    FONT-SIZE: 12px;
    text-align: left;
    white-Space: nowrap;
}
.th
{
    BORDER-RIGHT: #999999 2px solid;
    PADDING-RIGHT: 6px;
    PADDING-LEFT: 6px;
    FONT-WEIGHT: Bold;
```

```
    PADDING-BOTTOM: 6px;
    COLOR: black;
    PADDING-TOP: 6px;
    BORDER-BOTTOM: #999 2px solid;
    BACKGROUND-COLOR: #eeeeee;
    FONT-FAMILY: font-family: Cambria, serif;
    FONT-SIZE: 10px;
    text-align: right;
    white-Space: nowrap;
}
td
{
    BORDER-RIGHT: #999999 3px solid;
    PADDING-RIGHT: 6px;
    PADDING-LEFT: 6px;
    FONT-WEIGHT: Normal;
    PADDING-BOTTOM: 6px;
    COLOR: navy;
    LINE-HEIGHT: 14px;
    PADDING-TOP: 6px;
    BORDER-BOTTOM: #999 1px solid;
    BACKGROUND-COLOR: #eeeeee;
    FONT-FAMILY: font-family: Cambria, serif;
    FONT-SIZE: 12px;
    text-align: left;
    white-Space: nowrap;
}
div
{
    BORDER-RIGHT: #999999 3px solid;
    PADDING-RIGHT: 6px;
    PADDING-LEFT: 6px;
    FONT-WEIGHT: Normal;
    PADDING-BOTTOM: 6px;
    COLOR: white;
    PADDING-TOP: 6px;
    BORDER-BOTTOM: #999 1px solid;
    BACKGROUND-COLOR: navy;
    FONT-FAMILY: font-family: Cambria, serif;
    FONT-SIZE: 10px;
```

```
      text-align: left;
      white-Space: nowrap;
}
span
{
      BORDER-RIGHT: #999999 3px solid;
      PADDING-RIGHT: 3px;
      PADDING-LEFT: 3px;
      FONT-WEIGHT: Normal;
      PADDING-BOTTOM: 3px;
      COLOR: white;
      PADDING-TOP: 3px;
      BORDER-BOTTOM: #999 1px solid;
      BACKGROUND-COLOR: navy;
      FONT-FAMILY: font-family: Cambria, serif;
      FONT-SIZE: 10px;
      text-align: left;
      white-Space: nowrap;
      display: inline-block;
      width: 100%;
}
textarea
{
      BORDER-RIGHT: #999999 3px solid;
      PADDING-RIGHT: 3px;
      PADDING-LEFT: 3px;
      FONT-WEIGHT: Normal;
      PADDING-BOTTOM: 3px;
      COLOR: white;
      PADDING-TOP: 3px;
      BORDER-BOTTOM: #999 1px solid;
      BACKGROUND-COLOR: navy;
      FONT-FAMILY: font-family: Cambria, serif;
      FONT-SIZE: 12px;
      text-align: left;
      width: 100%;
}
select
{
      BORDER-RIGHT: #999999 1px solid;
```

```
    PADDING-RIGHT: 1px;
    PADDING-LEFT: 1px;
    FONT-WEIGHT: Normal;
    PADDING-BOTTOM: 1px;
    COLOR: white;
    PADDING-TOP: 1px;
    BORDER-BOTTOM: #999 1px solid;
    BACKGROUND-COLOR: navy;
    FONT-FAMILY: Cambria, serif;
    FONT-SIZE: 12px;
    text-align: left;
    white-Space: nowrap;
    width: 450px;
}
select1
{
    BORDER-RIGHT: #999999 1px solid;
    PADDING-RIGHT: 1px;
    PADDING-LEFT: 1px;
    FONT-WEIGHT: Normal;
    PADDING-BOTTOM: 1px;
    COLOR: white;
    PADDING-TOP: 1px;
    BORDER-BOTTOM: #999 1px solid;
    BACKGROUND-COLOR: navy;
    FONT-FAMILY: Cambria, serif;
    FONT-SIZE: 12px;
    text-align: left;
    white-Space: nowrap;
    width: 450px;
}
select2
{
    BORDER-RIGHT: #999999 1px solid;
    PADDING-RIGHT: 1px;
    PADDING-LEFT: 1px;
    FONT-WEIGHT: Normal;
    PADDING-BOTTOM: 1px;
    COLOR: white;
    PADDING-TOP: 1px;
```

```css
    BORDER-BOTTOM: #999 1px solid;
    BACKGROUND-COLOR: navy;
    FONT-FAMILY: Cambria, serif;
    FONT-SIZE: 12px;
    text-align: left;
    white-Space: nowrap;
    width: 450px;
}
#select
{
    BORDER-RIGHT: #999999 1px solid;
    PADDING-RIGHT: 1px;
    PADDING-LEFT: 1px;
    FONT-WEIGHT: Normal;
    PADDING-BOTTOM: 1px;
    COLOR: white;
    PADDING-TOP: 1px;
    BORDER-BOTTOM: #999 1px solid;
    BACKGROUND-COLOR: navy;
    FONT-FAMILY: Cambria, serif;
    FONT-SIZE: 12px;
    text-align: left;
    white-Space: nowrap;
    width: 100px;
}
select4
{
    BORDER-RIGHT: #999999 1px solid;
    PADDING-RIGHT: 1px;
    PADDING-LEFT: 1px;
    FONT-WEIGHT: Normal;
    PADDING-BOTTOM: 1px;
    COLOR: white;
    PADDING-TOP: 1px;
    BORDER-BOTTOM: #999 1px solid;
    BACKGROUND-COLOR: navy;
    FONT-FAMILY: Cambria, serif;
    FONT-SIZE: 12px;
    text-align: left;
    white-Space: nowrap;
```

```
        width: 254px;
    }
    input
    {
        BORDER-RIGHT: #999999 3px solid;
        PADDING-RIGHT: 3px;
        PADDING-LEFT: 3px;
        FONT-WEIGHT: Bold;
        PADDING-BOTTOM: 3px;
        COLOR: white;
        PADDING-TOP: 3px;
        BORDER-BOTTOM: #999 1px solid;
        BACKGROUND-COLOR: navy;
        FONT-FAMILY: font-family: Cambria, serif;
        FONT-SIZE: 12px;
        text-align: left;
        display: table-cell;
        white-Space: nowrap;
        width: 100%;
    }
    </style>
    <body BGColor=#242424>
    <table         style="Position:Absolute;Top:0px;Left:0px;Width:900px;Font-
family:Tahoma;font-size:10px">
    <tr><th  class=tdbackground  align=Right  Width=100px  nowrap>Required
Options</th>
    <th align=right style="Width:77px;" nowrap><b>Filename:</b></th>
    <td   align=left   nowrap><input   Type='text'   id='FName'   name='FName'
style='width:750px;'></input></td>
    <td><input        Type='Button'        id='Search'        name='Search'
style='width:50px;Background-color:ButtonFace;color:black;'
Value="Go!"></input></td>
    </tr>
    <tr>
    <tr><th class=tdbackground align=Right Width=115px nowrap> </th>
    <th align=right Width=77px nowrap><b>Tables: </b></th>
    <td    align=left    nowrap><select    id="trex"    style="width:125px;background-
Color:navy;Color:White;"                 onChange="HandlestrexChange()"
name="trexPullDown"></select>
```

```html
        Custom    Query: <input    Type='text'    id='CQuery'    name=CQuery'
style='width:540px;'></input>
        </td>
        <td><input Type='Button' id='LT1' name='LT1' style='width:50px;Background-
color:ButtonFace;color:black;' Value="Go!"></input></td></tr>
        </table>

        <table         style="Position:Absolute;Top:100px;Left:0px;Width:900px;Font-
family:Tahoma;font-size:10px">
        <tr><th class=tdbackground align=Center nowrap>Additional Options</th>
        <th       class="myclass"       Style="color:Black;font-family:Tahoma;font-
size:12px;width:115px;" Align=Right Nowrap>ADO Coding:</TH>
        <th><SELECT          ID="ADOCoding"          class="myclass1"
style="width:195px;background-Color:navy;Color:White"
onChange="HandlesEngineTypeChange()" name="EngineTypePullDown">
        <option Value="*Select A CodingType*">*Select A CodingType*</option>
        <option Value="cncmdrs">Connection Command And Recordset</option>
        <option Value="cnrs">Connection And Recordset</option>
        <option Value="cmdrs">Command And Recordset</option>
        <option Value="rs">Recordset</option>
        </SELECT></th>
        <th       class="myclass"       Style="color:Black;font-family:Tahoma;font-
size:12px;width:115px;" Align=Right Nowrap>html ADO Coding:</TH>
        <th><SELECT          ID="HTMLADOCoding"          class="myclass1"
style="width:195px;background-Color:navy;Color:White"
onChange="HandlesHTMLEngineTypeChange()"
name="HTMLEngineTypePullDown">
        <option    Value="*Select    An    HTMLCodingType*">*Select    An
HTMLCodingType*</option>
        <option Value="cncmdrs">Connection Command And Recordset</option>
        <option Value="cnrs">Connection And Recordset</option>
        <option Value="cmdrs">Command And Recordset</option>
        <option Value="rs">Recordset</option>
        </SELECT></th>
        <th       class="myclass"       Style="color:Black;font-family:Tahoma;font-
size:12px;width:115px;" Align=Right Nowrap>TableType:</TH>
        <th><SELECT          ID="TableType"          class="myclass1"
style="width:125px;background-Color:navy;Color:White"
onChange="HandlesTableTypeChange()" name="TableTypePullDown">
        <option Value="*Select A TableType*">*Select An Option*</option>
```

```html
<option Value="Table">Table</option>
<option Value="Report">Report</option>
</SELECT></th>
</tr>
<tr>
<th class=tdbackground align=Center nowrap> </th><th class="myclass" Style="color:Black;font-family:Tahoma;font-size:12px" Align=Right nowrap> Orientation:</TH>
<th>
<SELECT class="myclass1" style="width:125px;background-Color:navy;Color:White" onChange="HandlesOrientationChange()" name="OrientationPullDown">
<option selected Value="*Select An Orientation*">*Select An Option*</option>
<option Value="Multi-Line Horizontal">Multi-Line Horizontal</option>
<option Value="Multi-Line Vertical">Multi-Line Vertical</option>
<option Value="Single-Line Horizontal">Single-Line Horizontal</option>
<option Value="Single-Line Vertical">Single-Line Vertical</option>
</SELECT></TH>
<TH class="myclass" Style="color:Black;font-family:Tahoma;font-size:12px" Align=Right nowrap> Additional Tags:</TH>
<TH>
<SELECT class="myclass1" style="width:125px;background-Color:navy;Color:White" onChange="HandlesControlTypeChange()" name="ControlTypePullDown">
<option selected Value="*Select An Additional Tag*">*Select An Option*</option>
<option Value="Button">Button</option>
<option Value="Combobox">Combobox</option>
<option Value="Div">Div</option>
<option Value="Listbox">Listbox</option>
<option Value="Span">Span</option>
<option Value="Textarea">Textarea</option>
<option Value="Textbox">Textbox</option>
</SELECT></TH>
<TH class="myclass" Style="color:Black;font-family:Tahoma;font-size:12px" Align=Right nowrap> StyleSheets:</TH>
<TH>
<SELECT class="myclass" style="width:125px;background-Color:navy;Color:White" onChange="HandlesStyleSheetChange()" name="StyleSheetPullDown">
```

```html
<option selected Value="*Select A StyleSheet*">*Select An Option*</option>
<option Value="None">None</option>
<option Value="Basic">Basic</option>
<option Value="InLine">InLine</option>
<option Value="BlackAndWhiteText">Black And White Text</option>
<option Value="OscillatingRowColors">Oscillating Row Colors</option>
<option Value="ColoredText">Colored Text</option>
<option Value="GhostDecorated">Ghost Decorated</Option>
<option Value="3D">3d</option>
<option Value="ShadowBox">Shadow Box</option>
<option Value="Customized">Customized</options>
</select></TH></TR>
</table>
<table          style="Position:Absolute;Top:190px;Left:0px;Width:400px;Font-family:Tahoma;font-size:10px">
<tr><th          class="myclass"          Style="background-Color:buttonface;color:darkred;font-family:Tahoma;font-size:12px;Width:115px" Align=Right nowrap>Binding Types:</th>
<th   Style="background-Color:buttonface;color:Black;font-family:Tahoma;font-size:12px" Align=Right nowrap>Static</th>
<th><input          type='checkbox'          id='st'          name='st'          checked=true style="width:25px;background-Color:buttonface;Color:black"></input></th>
<th   Style="background-Color:buttonface;color:Black;font-family:Tahoma;font-size:12px" Align=Right nowrap>Dynamic</th>
<th><input          type='checkbox'          id='dynamic'          name='dynamic' style="width:25px;background-Color:buttonface;Color:black"></input></th>
<th   Style="background-Color:buttonface;color:Black;font-family:Tahoma;font-size:12px" Align=Right nowrap>Cloaked</th>
<th><input          type='checkbox'          id='cloaked'          name='cloaked' style="width:25px;background-Color:buttonface;Color:black"></input></th>
<th   Style="background-Color:buttonface;color:Black;font-family:Tahoma;font-size:12px" Align=Right nowrap>Bound</th>
<th><input          type='checkbox'          id='bound'          name='bound' style="width:25px;background-Color:buttonface;Color:black"></input></th>
</tr>
</table>
<table   style="Position:Absolute;Top:245px;Left:0px;Font-family:Tahoma;font-size:10px">
<TR><TH          class=td          background          align=Center          nowrap colspan=6>Checks</TH></TR>
```

```
<TR>
<TH align=left nowrap>
<input          Type='Button'          id='Providers'          name='Providers'
style='width:150px;Background-color:ButtonFace;color:black;'          Value="List
Providers"></input>
</TH></TR>
<TR>
<TH align=left nowrap>
<input          Type='Button'          id='ISAMS'          name='ISAMS'
style='width:150px;Background-color:ButtonFace;color:black;' Value="List Installed
ISAMS"></input>
</TH></TR>
<TR>
<TH align=left nowrap">
<input          Type='Button'          id='Drivers'          name='Drivers'
style='width:150px;Background-color:ButtonFace;color:black;' Value="List Installed
Drivers"></input>
</th></tr>
<TR>
<TH align=left nowrap>
<input          Type='Button'          id='DataLinks1'          name='DataLinks1'
style='width:150px;Background-color:ButtonFace;color:black;'          Value="Use
Connection Helper"></input>
</TH></TR>
<TR>
<TH align=left nowrap">
<input          Type='Button'          id='Createtemplate'          name='CreateTemplate'
style='width:150px;Background-color:ButtonFace;color:black;'          Value="Create
Template"></input>
</TH></TR>
<TH align=left nowrap>
<input          Type='Button'          id='UseTemplate'          name='UseTemplate'
style='width:150px;Background-color:ButtonFace;color:black;'          Value="Use
Template"></input>
</TH></TR>
<TR><TH          class=td          background          align=Center          nowrap
colspan=5>Actions</TH></TR>
<TR>
<TH align=left nowrap>
```

```html
    <input          Type='Button'          id='Clipboard1'          name='Clipboard1'
style='width:150px;Background-color:ButtonFace;color:black;'     Value="Copy     To
Clipboard"></input>
    </TH>
    </TR>
    <TR>
    <TH align=left nowrap>
    <input          Type='Button'          id='RunMe'          name='RunMe'
style='width:150px;Background-color:ButtonFace;color:black;'          Value="Run
Code"></input>
    </TH></TR>
    <TR>
    <TH align=left nowrap>
    <input          Type='Button'          id='ViewMe'          name='ViewMe'
style='width:150px;Background-color:ButtonFace;color:black;'          Value="View
Results"></input>
    </TH></TR>
    <TR>
    <TH align=left nowrap>
    <input          Type='Button'          id='Document'          name='Documenter'
style='width:150px;Background-color:ButtonFace;color:black;'          Value="Use
Documented Code"></input>
    </TH></TR>

    <TR><TH    align=left    nowrap><input    Type='Button'    id='wd'    name='wd'
style='width:150px;Background-color:ButtonFace;color:black;'    Value="Create    Word
Document"></input></TH></TR>

    <TR>
    <TH align=left nowrap>
    <input          Type='Button'          id='EMAIL'          name='EMAIL'
style='width:150px;Background-color:ButtonFace;color:black;'          Value="E-Mail
Results"></input>
    </TH></TR>
    </table>
    </table>

    <TABLE                    style="Position:Absolute;Top:245px;Left:180px;Font-
family:Tahoma;font-size:10px">
    <TR><TH>
```

```
<v:roundrect id="A" style="width:120;height:30px" arcsize="5%">
<v:fill color="#CCCCCC" color2="white" Opacity=90% Opacity2=90%
method="linear sigma" angle="-135" type="gradientradial" />
<v:textbox id="A1" style="font-family:Garmond;Font-
size:12px;Color:darkred"><b>The Code</b></v:textbox>
<v:shadow id="A2" on="false" offset="3pt, 3pt" opacity="70%"
color="black"/>
</v:roundrect>
</TH></TR>
</TABLE>
<TABLE style="border:solid;border-color:Blue;border-
width:1px;Position:Absolute;Left:180;Top:285px;width:832px;Height:505px">
<TR><TH><Textarea ID="Textarea1" name="Textarea1" Style="font-
family:Courier New;Height:505px;Width:832px;"
wrap="off"></textarea></TH></TR>
</TABLE>


<Table class="myclass" Style="border:outset;border-color:Silver;border-
width:1px;position:absolute;top:820px;left:0px;">
<tr><th class=tdbackground align=Center nowrap colspan=10>Required E-MAIL
Properties</th></tr>
<TR><TH class="myclass" Style="color:Black;font-family:Tahoma;font-
size:10px" Align=Right Nowrap>ServerName:</TH>
<th>
<Input type='text' id=sn style="width:150px;background-
Color:navy;Color:White"></input>
</th>
<th class="myclass" Style="color:Black;font-family:Tahoma;font-size:10px"
Align=Right nowrap>LoginUser:</TH>
<th>
<Input type='text' id=lnu style="width:150px;background-
Color:navy;Color:White"></input>
</TH>
<TH class="myclass" Style="color:Black;font-family:Tahoma;font-size:10px"
Align=Right nowrap>Password:</TH>
<TH>
<Input type='password' id=lpwd style="width:150px;background-
Color:navy;Color:White"></input>
</TH>
```

```
<TH class="myclass" Style="color:Black;font-family:Tahoma;font-size:10px"
Align=Right nowrap>Your Mail Name:</TH>
<TH>
<Input type='text' id=emfn style="width:150px;background-
Color:navy;Color:White"></input>
</TH>
</TR>
<TR><TH class="myclass" Style="color:Black;font-family:Tahoma;font-
size:10px" Align=Right Nowrap>Your Mail Address:</TH>
<th>
<Input type='text' id=ema style="width:150px;background-
Color:navy;Color:White"></input>
</th>
<th class="myclass" Style="color:Black;font-family:Tahoma;font-size:10px"
Align=Right nowrap>Sending it to:</TH>
<th>
<Input type='text' id="rec" style="width:150px;background-
Color:navy;Color:White"></input>
</TH>
<TH class="myclass" Style="color:Black;font-family:Tahoma;font-size:10px"
Align=Right nowrap>Subject</TH>
<TH colspan=4>
<Input type='text' id=s style="width:415px;background-
Color:navy;Color:White"></input>
</TH>
</TR>
</table>


<script language="vbscript">

Dim cnstr
Dim cn
Dim Provider
Dim rs

Dim EngineConfiguration
Dim HTMLEngineConfiguration
Dim txtstream
Dim TableType
```

```
Dim Orientation
Dim ControlType
Dim Filename
Dim strQuery
Dim Tablename
Dim Value
Dim StyleSheet


Provider="Microsoft.ACE.OleDb.15.0"

Filename = ""
strQuery = ""
Tablename = ""

EngineConfiguration = "rs"
HTMLEngineConfiguration = "rs"
TableType = "Table"
Orientation = "Multi-Line Horizontal"
ControlType = "Span"
StyleSheet = "InLine"

Sub Window_onLoad()

    window.moveTo 0, 0
    window.resizeTo 1055, 975
    RunMe.Disabled = true

End Sub

Sub HandlesEngineTypeChange()

    If EngineTypePullDown.Value <> "*Select An Option*" then

        EngineConfiguration = EngineTypePullDown.Value

    End If

End sub
```

```
Sub HandlesHTMLEngineTypeChange()

    If HTMLEngineTypePullDown.Value <> "*Select An Option*" then

        HTMLEngineConfiguration = HTMLEngineTypePullDown.Value

    End If

End sub

Sub st_OnClick()
    If st.Checked = true then
        dynamic.Checked = false
        cloaked.Checked = false
        bound.Checked = false
        If trexPullDown.Value <> "*Select An Option*" then
            Write_The_Code
        End If
    End If
End Sub

Sub dynamic_OnClick()
    If dynamic.Checked = true then
        st.Checked = false
        cloaked.Checked = false
        bound.Checked = false
        If trexPullDown.Value <> "*Select An Option*" then
            Write_The_Code
        End If
    End If
End Sub

Sub cloaked_OnClick()
    If cloaked.Checked = true then
        dynamic.Checked = false
        st.Checked = false
        bound.Checked = false
        If trexPullDown.Value <> "*Select An Option*" then
            Write_The_Code
        End If
```

```
    End If
End Sub

Sub bound_OnClick()
  If bound.Checked = true then
    dynamic.Checked = false
    cloaked.Checked = false
    st.Checked = false
    If trexPullDown.Value <> "*Select An Option*" then
       Write_The_Code
    End If
  End If
End Sub


Sub HandlesTableTypeChange()

  If TableTypePullDown.Value <> "*Select A TableType*" Then
    TableType = TableTypePullDown.Value
    Write_The_Code

  End If

End Sub


Sub HandlestrexChange()

  If trexPullDown.Value <> "*Select An Option*" then

    dim pos
    pos = instr(trexPullDown.Value, " ")
    if pos > 0 then
       CQuery.Value = "Select * From [" & trexPullDown.Value & "]"
    else
       CQuery.Value = "Select * From " & trexPullDown.Value
    End If

  End If
```

```
End Sub


Sub HandlesOrientationChange()

  If OrientationPullDown.Value <> "*Select An Orientation*" Then
    Orientation = OrientationPullDown.Value
    Write_The_Code
  End If

End Sub

Sub HandlesControlTypeChange()

  If ControlTypePullDown.Value <> "*Select An Additional Tag*" Then
    ControlType = ControlTypePullDown.Value
    Write_The_Code
  End If

End Sub

Sub HandlesStyleSheetChange()

If StyleSheetPullDown.Value <> "*Select A StyleSheet*" Then
    StyleSheet = StyleSheetPullDown.Value
    Write_The_Code
End If

End Sub

Sub Write_The_Code()

    textarea1.innerText = ""

    If FName.Value = "" then
       msgbox("Please provide the location and name of the database you want
to use before clicking here.")
       exit sub
    else
       Filename = FName.Value
```

```
End If

If CQuery.Value = "" then
   msgbox("Please create a Query string before clicking here.")
   exit sub
End If

strQuery = CQuery.Value

dim pos
pos = instr(trexPullDown.Value, " ")
if pos > 0 then
   Tablename = Replace(trexPullDown.Value, " ", "_")
else
   Tablename = trexPullDown.Value
End If

if st.Checked = True then
   Do_Static
   Exit Sub

End If

if dynamic.Checked = True then

   Do_Dynamic
   Exit Sub

End If

if cloaked.Checked = True then

   Do_Cloaked
   Exit Sub

End If

if bound.Checked = True then

   Do_Bound
```

```
        Exit Sub

    End If

End sub

Sub Do_Static()

  Select Case EngineConfiguration

    Case "cncmdrs"

            Set cn = CreateObject("ADODB.Connection")
            Set cmd = CreateObject("ADODB.Command")
            Set rs = CreateObject("ADODB.Recordset")


            cn.ConnectionString = "Provider=" & Provider & ";Data Source=" &
fName.Value & ";"
            Call cn.Open()

            cmd.ActiveConnection = cn
            cmd.CommandType = 8
            cmd.CommandText = strQuery
            Call cmd.Execute()

            rs.CursorLocation = 3
            rs.LockType = 3
            Call rs.Open(cmd)


    Case "cnrs"

            Set cn = CreateObject("ADODB.Connection")
            Set rs = CreateObject("ADODB.Recordset")
```

```
            cn.ConnectionString = "Provider=" & Provider & ";Data Source=" &
fName.Value & ";"
            Call cn.Open()

            rs.ActiveConnection = cn
            rs.CursorLocation = 3
            rs.LockType = 3
            rs.Source = strQuery
            Call rs.Open()

        Case "cmdrs"

            Set cmd = CreateObject("ADODB.Command")
            Set rs = CreateObject("ADODB.Recordset")

            cmd.ActiveConnection = "Provider=" & Provider & ";Data Source=" &
fName.Value & ";"
            cmd.CommandType = 8
            cmd.CommandText = strQuery
            Call cmd.Execute()

            rs.CursorLocation = 3
            rs.LockType = 3
            Call rs.Open(cmd)

        Case "rs"

        Set rs = CreateObject("ADODB.Recordset")
            rs.ActiveConnection = "Provider=" & Provider & ";Data Source=" &
fName.Value & ";"
            rs.LockType = 3
            rs.Cursorlocation = 3
            rs.Source = strQuery
            Call rs.Open()

    End Select


        Set ws = CreateObject("WScript.Shell")
```

```
        Set fso = CreateObject("Scripting.FileSystemObject")

        Set txtstream = fso.OpenTextFile(ws.CurrentDirectory & "\" & tablename &
".html", 2, True, -2)
        txtstream.WriteLine("<html>")
        txtstream.WriteLine("<head>")
        txtstream.WriteLine("<title>" & Tablename & "</title>")

    Add_The_StyleSheet

        txtstream.WriteLine("</head>")
        txtstream.WriteLine("<body>")
        txtstream.WriteLine("")

        If StyleSheet = "InLine" Then


            Select Case Orientation


                Case "Single-Line Horizontal"

                    Select Case TableType

                        Case "Table"

                            txtstream.WriteLine("<table      Border='1'      cellpadding='1'
cellspacing='1' datasrc=#rs>")

                        Case "Report"

                            txtstream.WriteLine("<table      Border='0'      cellpadding='1'
cellspacing='1' datasrc=#rs>")

                    End Select


                    txtstream.WriteLine("<tr>")
                    For x = 0 To rs.Fields.Count - 1
```

```vb
            txtstream.WriteLine("<th      style='font-family:Calibri,      Sans-
Serif;font-size: 12px;color:darkred;'>" & rs.Fields(x).Name & "</th>")

        Next
        txtstream.WriteLine("</tr>")
        txtstream.WriteLine("<tr>")
        For x = 0 To rs.Fields.Count - 1


            Select Case ControlType

                Case "None"
                            txtstream.WriteLine("<td              style='font-
family:Calibri,  Sans-Serif;font-size:  12px;color:navy;'>"  &  rs.Fields(x).Value  &
"</td>")
                Case "Button"
                            txtstream.WriteLine("<td              style='font-
family:Calibri, Sans-Serif;font-size: 12px;color:navy;'><input type=button Value='"
& rs.Fields(x).Value & "'></input></td>")
                Case "Combobox"
                            txtstream.WriteLine("<td              style='font-
family:Calibri, Sans-Serif;font-size: 12px;color:navy;'><select><option Value='" &
rs.Fields(x).Value & "'>" & rs.Fields(x).Value & "</option></select></td>")
                Case "Div"
                            txtstream.WriteLine("<td              style='font-
family:Calibri, Sans-Serif;font-size: 12px;color:navy;'><div>" & rs.Fields(x).Value &
"</div></td>")
                Case "Listbox"
                            txtstream.WriteLine("<td              style='font-
family:Calibri,         Sans-Serif;font-size:         12px;color:navy;'><select
multiple=true><option Value ='" & rs.Fields(x).Value & "'>" & rs.Fields(x).Value &
"</option></select></td>")
                Case "Span"
                            txtstream.WriteLine("<td              style='font-
family:Calibri, Sans-Serif;font-size: 12px;color:navy;'><span>" & rs.Fields(x).Value
& "</span></td>")
                Case "Textbox"
                            txtstream.WriteLine("<td              style='font-
family:Calibri, Sans-Serif;font-size: 12px;color:navy;'><input type=text Value='" &
rs.Fields(x).Value & "'></input></td>")
```

```
            Case "Textarea"
                        txtstream.WriteLine("<td              style='font-
family:Calibri,     Sans-Serif;font-size:     12px;color:navy;'><textarea>"     &
rs.Fields(x).Value & "</textarea></td>")

        End Select


    Next

    txtstream.WriteLine("</tr>")


Case "Multi-Line Horizontal"


    Select Case TableType

        Case "Table"

            txtstream.WriteLine("<table        Border='1'       cellpadding='1'
cellspacing='1'>")

        Case "Report"

            txtstream.WriteLine("<table        Border='0'       cellpadding='1'
cellspacing='1'>")

    End Select

    txtstream.WriteLine("<tr>")
    For x = 0 To rs.Fields.Count - 1

            txtstream.WriteLine("<th       style='font-family:Calibri,      Sans-
Serif;font-size: 12px;color:darkred;'>" & rs.Fields(x).Name & "</th>")

        Next
        txtstream.WriteLine("</tr>")
        Do While rs.EOF = False
```

```
txtstream.WriteLine("<tr>")
For x = 0 To rs.Fields.Count - 1

    Select Case ControlType

        Case "None"
                        txtstream.WriteLine("<td    style='font-
family:Calibri,  Sans-Serif;font-size:  12px;color:navy;'>"  &  rs.Fields(x).Value  &
"</td>")
        Case "Button"
                        txtstream.WriteLine("<td    style='font-
family:Calibri, Sans-Serif;font-size: 12px;color:navy;'><input type=button Value='"
& rs.Fields(x).Value & "'></input></td>")
        Case "Combobox"
                        txtstream.WriteLine("<td    style='font-
family:Calibri, Sans-Serif;font-size: 12px;color:navy;'><select><option Value='" &
rs.Fields(x).Value & "'>" & rs.Fields(x).Value & "</option></select></td>")
        Case "Div"
                        txtstream.WriteLine("<td    style='font-
family:Calibri, Sans-Serif;font-size: 12px;color:navy;'><div>" & rs.Fields(x).Value &
"</div></td>")
        Case "Listbox"
                        txtstream.WriteLine("<td    style='font-
family:Calibri,          Sans-Serif;font-size:          12px;color:navy;'><select
multiple=true><option Value ='" & rs.Fields(x).Value & "'>" & rs.Fields(x).Value &
"</option></select></td>")
        Case "Span"
                        txtstream.WriteLine("<td    style='font-
family:Calibri, Sans-Serif;font-size: 12px;color:navy;'><span>" & rs.Fields(x).Value
& "</span></td>")
        Case "Textbox"
                        txtstream.WriteLine("<td    style='font-
family:Calibri, Sans-Serif;font-size: 12px;color:navy;'><input type=text Value='" &
rs.Fields(x).Value & "'></input></td>")
        Case "Textarea"
                        txtstream.WriteLine("<td    style='font-
family:Calibri,      Sans-Serif;font-size:      12px;color:navy;'><textarea>"      &
rs.Fields(x).Value & "</textarea></td>")
```

```
                End Select


            Next
            txtstream.WriteLine("</tr>")
            rs.MoveNext()
        Loop



    Case "Single-Line Vertical"


        Select Case TableType

            Case "Table"

                txtstream.WriteLine("<table        Border='1'        cellpadding='1'
cellspacing='1'>")

                Case "Report"

                txtstream.WriteLine("<table        Border='0'        cellpadding='1'
cellspacing='1'>")

            End Select

        For x = 0 To rs.Fields.Count - 1

            Select Case ControlType

                Case "None"
                            txtstream.WriteLine("<tr><th        style='font-
family:Calibri, Sans-Serif;font-size: 12px;color:darkred;'>" & rs.Fields(x).Name &
"</th><td style='font-family:Calibri, Sans-Serif;font-size: 12px;color:navy;'>" &
rs.Fields(x).Value & "</td></tr>")
                Case "Button"
                            txtstream.WriteLine("<tr><th        style='font-
family:Calibri, Sans-Serif;font-size: 12px;color:darkred;'>" & rs.Fields(x).Name &
```

```
"</th><td style='font-family:Calibri, Sans-Serif;font-size: 12px;color:navy;'><input
type=button Value='" & rs.Fields(x).Value & "'></input></td></tr>")
                Case "Combobox"
                        txtstream.WriteLine("<tr><th         style='font-
family:Calibri, Sans-Serif;font-size: 12px;color:darkred;'>" & rs.Fields(x).Name &
"</th>        <td         style='font-family:Calibri,      Sans-Serif;font-size:
12px;color:navy;'><select><option  Value='"  &  rs.Fields(x).Value  &  "'>"  &
rs.Fields(x).Value & "</option></select></td></tr>")
                Case "Div"
                        txtstream.WriteLine("<tr><th         style='font-
family:Calibri, Sans-Serif;font-size: 12px;color:darkred;'>" & rs.Fields(x).Name &
"</th><td style='font-family:Calibri, Sans-Serif;font-size: 12px;color:navy;'><div>"
& rs.Fields(x).Value & "</div></td></tr>")
                Case "Listbox"
                        txtstream.WriteLine("<tr><th         style='font-
family:Calibri, Sans-Serif;font-size: 12px;color:darkred;'>" & rs.Fields(x).Name &
"</th><td style='font-family:Calibri, Sans-Serif;font-size: 12px;color:navy;'><select
multiple=true><option Value ='" & rs.Fields(x).Value & "'>" & rs.Fields(x).Value &
"</option></select></td></tr>")
                Case "Span"
                        txtstream.WriteLine("<tr><th         style='font-
family:Calibri, Sans-Serif;font-size: 12px;color:darkred;'>" & rs.Fields(x).Name &
"</th><td         style='font-family:Calibri,         Sans-Serif;font-size:
12px;color:navy;'><span>" & rs.Fields(x).Value & "</span></td></tr>")
                Case "Textbox"
                        txtstream.WriteLine("<tr><th         style='font-
family:Calibri, Sans-Serif;font-size: 12px;color:darkred;'>" & rs.Fields(x).Name &
"</th><td style='font-family:Calibri, Sans-Serif;font-size: 12px;color:navy;'><input
type=text Value='" & rs.Fields(x).Value & "'></input></td></tr>")
                Case "Textarea"
                        txtstream.WriteLine("<tr><th         style='font-
family:Calibri, Sans-Serif;font-size: 12px;color:darkred;'>" & rs.Fields(x).Name &
"</th><td         style='font-family:Calibri,         Sans-Serif;font-size:
12px;color:navy;'><textarea>" & rs.Fields(x).Value & "</textarea></td></tr>")


        End Select


        Next
```

```
        Case "Multi-Line Vertical"

            Select Case TableType

                Case "Table"

                    txtstream.WriteLine("<table        Border='1'        cellpadding='1'
cellspacing='1'>")

                Case "Report"

                    txtstream.WriteLine("<table        Border='0'        cellpadding='1'
cellspacing='1'>")

            End Select


            For x = 0 To rs.Fields.Count - 1

                txtstream.WriteLine("<tr><th   style='font-family:Calibri,   Sans-
Serif;font-size: 12px;color:darkred;'>" & rs.Fields(x).Name & "</th>")

            rs.MoveFirst()

            Do While rs.EOF = False


                Select Case ControlType

                    Case "None"
                                txtstream.WriteLine("<td   style='font-
family:Calibri,   Sans-Serif;font-size:   12px;color:navy;'>"  &  rs.Fields(x).Value  &
"</td>")
                    Case "Button"
                                txtstream.WriteLine("<td   style='font-
family:Calibri, Sans-Serif;font-size: 12px;color:navy;'><input type=button Value='"
& rs.Fields(x).Value & "'></input></td>")
                    Case "Combobox"
```

```vb
                                txtstream.WriteLine("<td    style='font-
family:Calibri, Sans-Serif;font-size: 12px;color:navy;'><select><option Value='" &
rs.Fields(x).Value & "'>" & rs.Fields(x).Value & "</option></select></td>")
                Case "Div"
                                        txtstream.WriteLine("<td    style='font-
family:Calibri, Sans-Serif;font-size: 12px;color:navy;'><div>" & rs.Fields(x).Value &
"</div></td>")
                Case "Listbox"
                                        txtstream.WriteLine("<td    style='font-
family:Calibri,            Sans-Serif;font-size:          12px;color:navy;'><select
multiple=true><option Value ='" & rs.Fields(x).Value & "'>" & rs.Fields(x).Value &
"</option></select></td>")
                Case "Span"
                                        txtstream.WriteLine("<td    style='font-
family:Calibri, Sans-Serif;font-size: 12px;color:navy;'><span>" & rs.Fields(x).Value
& "</span></td>")
                Case "Textbox"
                                        txtstream.WriteLine("<td    style='font-
family:Calibri, Sans-Serif;font-size: 12px;color:navy;'><input type=text Value='" &
rs.Fields(x).Value & "'></input></td>")
                Case "Textarea"
                                        txtstream.WriteLine("<td    style='font-
family:Calibri,        Sans-Serif;font-size:        12px;color:navy;'><textarea>"        &
rs.Fields(x).Value & "</textarea></td>")

            End Select

            rs.MoveNext()

        Loop

        txtstream.WriteLine("</tr>")

    Next


    End Select
```

```
        Else

            Select Case Orientation

                Case "Single-Line Horizontal"

                Select Case TableType

                    Case "Table"

                        txtstream.WriteLine("<table        Border='1'        cellpadding='1'
cellspacing='1' datasrc=#rs>")

                        Case "Report"

                        txtstream.WriteLine("<table        Border='0'        cellpadding='1'
cellspacing='1' datasrc=#rs>")

                End Select

                txtstream.WriteLine("<tr>")
                For x = 0 To rs.Fields.Count - 1

                    txtstream.WriteLine("<th>" & rs.Fields(x).Name & "</th>")

                Next
                txtstream.WriteLine("</tr>")
                txtstream.WriteLine("<tr>")
                For x = 0 To rs.Fields.Count - 1


                    Select Case ControlType

                        Case "None"
                                    txtstream.WriteLine("<td>" & rs.Fields(x).Value
& "</td>")
                        Case "Button"
```

```vb
                    txtstream.WriteLine("<td><input    type=button
Value='" & rs.Fields(x).Value & "'></input></td>")
                Case "Combobox"
                    txtstream.WriteLine("<td><select><option
Value='"   &   rs.Fields(x).Value   &   "'>"   &   rs.Fields(x).Value   &
"</option></select></td>")
                Case "Div"
                    txtstream.WriteLine("<td><div>"                    &
rs.Fields(x).Value & "</div></td>")
                Case "Listbox"
                    txtstream.WriteLine("<td><select
multiple=true><option Value ='" & rs.Fields(x).Value & "'>" & rs.Fields(x).Value &
"</option></select></td>")
                Case "Span"
                    txtstream.WriteLine("<td><span>"                   &
rs.Fields(x).Value & "</span></td>")
                Case "Textbox"
                    txtstream.WriteLine("<td><input    type=text
Value='" & rs.Fields(x).Value & "'></input></td>")
                Case "Textarea"
                    txtstream.WriteLine("<td><textarea>"               &
rs.Fields(x).Value & "</textarea></td>")

        End Select


        Next

        txtstream.WriteLine("</tr>")


    Case "Multi-Line Horizontal"


        Select Case TableType

        Case "Table"
```

```
                    txtstream.WriteLine("<table        Border='1'        cellpadding='1'
cellspacing='1'>")

            Case "Report"

                    txtstream.WriteLine("<table        Border='0'        cellpadding='1'
cellspacing='1'>")

        End Select

        txtstream.WriteLine("<tr>")
        For x = 0 To rs.Fields.Count - 1

            txtstream.WriteLine("<th>" & rs.Fields(x).Name & "</th>")

        Next
        txtstream.WriteLine("</tr>")
        Do While rs.EOF = False

            txtstream.WriteLine("<tr>")
            For x = 0 To rs.Fields.Count - 1

            Select Case ControlType

                Case "None"
                                    txtstream.WriteLine("<td>"              &
rs.Fields(x).Value & "</td>")
                Case "Button"
                                    txtstream.WriteLine("<td><input
type=button Value='" & rs.Fields(x).Value & "'></input></td>")
                Case "Combobox"

            txtstream.WriteLine("<td><select><option Value='" & rs.Fields(x).Value &
"'>" & rs.Fields(x).Value & "</option></select></td>")
                Case "Div"
                                    txtstream.WriteLine("<td><div>"          &
rs.Fields(x).Value & "</div></td>")
                Case "Listbox"
```

```
                                        txtstream.WriteLine("<td><select
multiple=true><option Value ='" & rs.Fields(x).Value & "'>" & rs.Fields(x).Value &
"</option></select></td>")
                        Case "Span"
                                        txtstream.WriteLine("<td><span>"    &
rs.Fields(x).Value & "</span></td>")
                        Case "Textbox"
                                        txtstream.WriteLine("<td><input
type=text Value='" & rs.Fields(x).Value & "'></input></td>")
                        Case "Textarea"
                                        txtstream.WriteLine("<td><textarea>"
& rs.Fields(x).Value & "</textarea></td>")

                End Select


            Next
            txtstream.WriteLine("</tr>")
            rs.MoveNext()
        Loop


        Case "Single-Line Vertical"


        Select Case TableType

        Case "Table"

                txtstream.WriteLine("<table        Border='1'      cellpadding='1'
cellspacing='1'>")

        Case "Report"

                txtstream.WriteLine("<table        Border='0'      cellpadding='1'
cellspacing='1'>")

        End Select
```

```
For x = 0 To rs.Fields.Count - 1

    Select Case ControlType

        Case "None"
                        txtstream.WriteLine("<tr><th>"                    &
rs.Fields(x).Name & "</th><td>" & rs.Fields(x).Value & "</td></tr>")
        Case "Button"
                        txtstream.WriteLine("<tr><th>"                    &
rs.Fields(x).Name & "</th><td><input type=button Value='" & rs.Fields(x).Value &
"'></input></td></tr>")
        Case "Combobox"
                        txtstream.WriteLine("<tr><th>"                    &
rs.Fields(x).Name & "</th> <td><select><option Value='" & rs.Fields(x).Value &
"'>" & rs.Fields(x).Value & "</option></select></td></tr>")
        Case "Div"
                        txtstream.WriteLine("<tr><th>"                    &
rs.Fields(x).Name & "</th><td><div>" & rs.Fields(x).Value & "</div></td></tr>")
        Case "Listbox"
                        txtstream.WriteLine("<tr><th>"                    &
rs.Fields(x).Name  &  "</th><td><select  multiple=true><option  Value  ='"  &
rs.Fields(x).Value & "'>" & rs.Fields(x).Value & "</option></select></td></tr>")
        Case "Span"
                        txtstream.WriteLine("<tr><th>"                    &
rs.Fields(x).Name       &       "</th><td><span>"       &       rs.Fields(x).Value       &
"</span></td></tr>")
        Case "Textbox"
                        txtstream.WriteLine("<tr><th>"                    &
rs.Fields(x).Name & "</th><td><input type=text Value='" & rs.Fields(x).Value &
"'></input></td></tr>")
        Case "Textarea"
                        txtstream.WriteLine("<tr><th>"                    &
rs.Fields(x).Name       &       "</th><td><textarea>"       &       rs.Fields(x).Value       &
"</textarea></td></tr>")

    End Select

Next
```

```vb
        Case "Multi-Line Vertical"

            Select Case TableType

                Case "Table"

                    txtstream.WriteLine("<table      Border='1'      cellpadding='1'
cellspacing='1'>")

                Case "Report"

                    txtstream.WriteLine("<table      Border='0'      cellpadding='1'
cellspacing='1'>")

            End Select


            For x = 0 To rs.Fields.Count - 1

                txtstream.WriteLine("<tr><th>" & rs.Fields(x).Name & "</th>")

                rs.MoveFirst()

                Do While rs.EOF = False


                    Select Case ControlType

                        Case "None"
                                            txtstream.WriteLine("<td>"              &
rs.Fields(x).Value & "</td>")
                        Case "Button"
                                            txtstream.WriteLine("<td><input
type=button Value='" & rs.Fields(x).Value & "'></input></td>")
                        Case "Combobox"

            txtstream.WriteLine("<td><select><option Value='" & rs.Fields(x).Value &
"'>" & rs.Fields(x).Value & "</option></select></td>")
                        Case "Div"
```

```vb
                                        txtstream.WriteLine("<td><div>"        &
rs.Fields(x).Value & "</div></td>")
                    Case "Listbox"
                                        txtstream.WriteLine("<td><select
multiple=true><option Value ='" & rs.Fields(x).Value & "'>" & rs.Fields(x).Value &
"</option></select></td>")
                    Case "Span"
                                        txtstream.WriteLine("<td><span>"        &
rs.Fields(x).Value & "</span></td>")
                    Case "Textbox"
                                        txtstream.WriteLine("<td><input
type=text Value='" & rs.Fields(x).Value & "'></input></td>")
                    Case "Textarea"
                                        txtstream.WriteLine("<td><textarea>"
& rs.Fields(x).Value & "</textarea></td>")

                End Select

                rs.MoveNext()

            Loop

            txtstream.WriteLine("</tr>")

        Next


        End Select


    End If

    txtstream.WriteLine("</table>")
    txtstream.WriteLine("</body>")
    txtstream.WriteLine("</html>")
    txtstream.Close
```

```
        tempstr = ""
        Set txtstream = fso.OpenTextFile(ws.CurrentDirectory & "\" & Tablename &
".html", 1, true, -2)
        Do While txtstream.AtEndOfStream = false
           tempstr = tempstr & txtstream.ReadLine()
           tempstr = tempstr & vbcrlf
        loop
        txtstream.Close
        textarea1.innerText = tempstr


    End Sub

    Sub Do_Dynamic()

      Select Case EngineConfiguration


        Case "cncmdrs"


              Set cn = CreateObject("ADODB.Connection")
              Set cmd = CreateObject("ADODB.Command")
              Set rs = CreateObject("ADODB.Recordset")


              cn.ConnectionString = "Provider=" & Provider & ";Data Source=" &
fName.Value & ";"
              Call cn.Open()

              cmd.ActiveConnection = cn
              cmd.CommandType = 8
              cmd.CommandText = strQuery
              Call cmd.Execute()

              rs.CursorLocation = 3
              rs.LockType = 3
              Call rs.Open(cmd)
```

```
Case "cnrs"

        Set cn = CreateObject("ADODB.Connection")
        Set rs = CreateObject("ADODB.Recordset")

        cn.ConnectionString = "Provider=" & Provider & ";Data Source=" &
fName.Value & ";"
        Call cn.Open()

        rs.ActiveConnection = cn
        rs.CursorLocation = 3
        rs.LockType = 3
        rs.Source = strQuery
        Call rs.Open()

Case "cmdrs"

        Set cmd = CreateObject("ADODB.Command")
        Set rs = CreateObject("ADODB.Recordset")

        cmd.ActiveConnection = "Provider=" & Provider & ";Data Source=" &
fName.Value & ";"
        cmd.CommandType = 8
        cmd.CommandText = strQuery
        Call cmd.Execute()

        rs.CursorLocation = 3
        rs.LockType = 3
        Call rs.Open(cmd)

Case "rs"

    Set rs = CreateObject("ADODB.Recordset")
    rs.ActiveConnection = "Provider=" & Provider & ";Data Source=" &
fName.Value & ";"
        rs.LockType = 3
        rs.Cursorlocation = 3
        rs.Source = strQuery
        Call rs.Open()
```

```
        End Select

            Set ws = CreateObject("WScript.Shell")
            Set fso = CreateObject("Scripting.FileSystemObject")

            Set txtstream = fso.OpenTextFile(ws.CurrentDirectory & "\" & Tablename &
    ".html", 2, True, -2)
            txtstream.WriteLine ("<html>")
            txtstream.WriteLine ("<head>")
            txtstream.WriteLine ("<title>" & Tablename & "</title>")

        Add_The_StyleSheet

            txtstream.WriteLine ("</head>")
            txtstream.WriteLine ("<body>")
            txtstream.WriteLine ("<script language='vbscript'>")

            If StyleSheet = "InLine" Then


                Select Case Orientation


                    Case "Single-Line Horizontal"

                    Select Case TableType

                        Case "Table"

                            txtstream.WriteLine  ("document.WriteLn(""<table   Border='1'
    cellpadding='1' cellspacing='1' datasrc=#rs>"")")

                        Case "Report"

                            txtstream.WriteLine  ("document.WriteLn(""<table   Border='0'
    cellpadding='1' cellspacing='1' datasrc=#rs>"")")

                    End Select
```

```
txtstream.WriteLine ("document.WriteLn(""<tr>"")")
For x = 0 To rs.Fields.Count - 1

        txtstream.WriteLine    ("document.WriteLn(""<th    style='font-
family:Calibri, Sans-Serif;font-size: 12px;color:darkred;'>" & rs.Fields(x).Name &
"</th>"")")

    Next
    txtstream.WriteLine ("document.WriteLn(""</tr>"")")
    txtstream.WriteLine ("document.WriteLn(""<tr>"")")
    For x = 0 To rs.Fields.Count - 1


        Select Case ControlType

            Case "None"
            txtstream.WriteLine    ("document.WriteLn(""<td    style='font-
family:Calibri, Sans-Serif;font-size: 12px;color:navy;'>" & rs.Fields(x).Value &
"</td>"")")
            Case "Button"
            txtstream.WriteLine    ("document.WriteLn(""<td    style='font-
family:Calibri, Sans-Serif;font-size: 12px;color:navy;'><input type=button Value='"
& rs.Fields(x).Value & "'></input></td>"")")
            Case "Combobox"
            txtstream.WriteLine    ("document.WriteLn(""<td    style='font-
family:Calibri, Sans-Serif;font-size: 12px;color:navy;'><select><option Value='" &
rs.Fields(x).Value & "'>" & rs.Fields(x).Value & "</option></select></td>"")")
            Case "Div"
            txtstream.WriteLine    ("document.WriteLn(""<td    style='font-
family:Calibri, Sans-Serif;font-size: 12px;color:navy;'><div>" & rs.Fields(x).Value &
"</div></td>"")")
            Case "Listbox"
            txtstream.WriteLine    ("document.WriteLn(""<td    style='font-
family:Calibri,        Sans-Serif;font-size:        12px;color:navy;'><select
multiple=true><option Value ='" & rs.Fields(x).Value & "'>" & rs.Fields(x).Value &
"</option></select></td>"")")
            Case "Span"
            txtstream.WriteLine    ("document.WriteLn(""<td    style='font-
family:Calibri, Sans-Serif;font-size: 12px;color:navy;'><span>" & rs.Fields(x).Value
& "</span></td>"")")
```

```vb
                    Case "Textbox"
            txtstream.WriteLine        ("document.WriteLn(""<td        style='font-
family:Calibri, Sans-Serif;font-size: 12px;color:navy;'><input type=text Value='" &
rs.Fields(x).Value & "'></input></td>"")")
                    Case "Textarea"
            txtstream.WriteLine        ("document.WriteLn(""<td        style='font-
family:Calibri,      Sans-Serif;font-size:      12px;color:navy;'><textarea>"      &
rs.Fields(x).Value & "</textarea></td>"")")

        End Select



        Next

        txtstream.WriteLine ("document.WriteLn(""</tr>"")")


    Case "Multi-Line Horizontal"


        Select Case TableType

        Case "Table"

            txtstream.WriteLine    ("document.WriteLn(""<table    Border='1'
cellpadding='1' cellspacing='1'>"")")

        Case "Report"

            txtstream.WriteLine    ("document.WriteLn(""<table    Border='0'
cellpadding='1' cellspacing='1'>"")")

        End Select

        txtstream.WriteLine ("document.WriteLn(""<tr>"")")
        For x = 0 To rs.Fields.Count - 1
```

```
                txtstream.WriteLine    ("document.WriteLn(""<th    style='font-
family:Calibri, Sans-Serif;font-size: 12px;color:darkred;'>" & rs.Fields(x).Name &
"</th>"")")

            Next
            txtstream.WriteLine ("document.WriteLn(""</tr>"")")
            Do While rs.EOF = False

                txtstream.WriteLine ("document.WriteLn(""<tr>"")")
                For x = 0 To rs.Fields.Count - 1

                Select Case ControlType

                    Case "None"
                    txtstream.WriteLine    ("document.WriteLn(""<td    style='font-
family:Calibri, Sans-Serif;font-size: 12px;color:navy;'>" & rs.Fields(x).Value &
"</td>"")")
                    Case "Button"
                    txtstream.WriteLine    ("document.WriteLn(""<td    style='font-
family:Calibri, Sans-Serif;font-size: 12px;color:navy;'><input type=button Value='"
& rs.Fields(x).Value & "'></input></td>"")")
                    Case "Combobox"
                    txtstream.WriteLine    ("document.WriteLn(""<td    style='font-
family:Calibri, Sans-Serif;font-size: 12px;color:navy;'><select><option Value='" &
rs.Fields(x).Value & "'>" & rs.Fields(x).Value & "</option></select></td>"")")
                    Case "Div"
                    txtstream.WriteLine    ("document.WriteLn(""<td    style='font-
family:Calibri, Sans-Serif;font-size: 12px;color:navy;'><div>" & rs.Fields(x).Value &
"</div></td>"")")
                    Case "Listbox"
                    txtstream.WriteLine    ("document.WriteLn(""<td    style='font-
family:Calibri,         Sans-Serif;font-size:         12px;color:navy;'><select
multiple=true><option Value ='" & rs.Fields(x).Value & "'>" & rs.Fields(x).Value &
"</option></select></td>"")")
                    Case "Span"
                    txtstream.WriteLine    ("document.WriteLn(""<td    style='font-
family:Calibri, Sans-Serif;font-size: 12px;color:navy;'><span>" & rs.Fields(x).Value
& "</span></td>"")")
                    Case "Textbox"
```

```
                txtstream.WriteLine    ("document.WriteLn(""<td    style='font-
family:Calibri, Sans-Serif;font-size: 12px;color:navy;'><input type=text Value='" &
rs.Fields(x).Value & "'></input></td>"")")
                Case "Textarea"
                txtstream.WriteLine    ("document.WriteLn(""<td    style='font-
family:Calibri,    Sans-Serif;font-size:    12px;color:navy;'><textarea>"    &
rs.Fields(x).Value & "</textarea></td>"")")

            End Select


        Next
        txtstream.WriteLine ("document.WriteLn(""</tr>"")")
        rs.MoveNext
    Loop



    Case "Single-Line Vertical"


    Select Case TableType

        Case "Table"

            txtstream.WriteLine    ("document.WriteLn(""<table    Border='1'
cellpadding='1' cellspacing='1'>"")")

        Case "Report"

            txtstream.WriteLine    ("document.WriteLn(""<table    Border='0'
cellpadding='1' cellspacing='1'>"")")

    End Select

    For x = 0 To rs.Fields.Count - 1

        Select Case ControlType

            Case "None"
```

```
            txtstream.WriteLine      ("document.WriteLn(""""<tr><th      style='font-
family:Calibri, Sans-Serif;font-size: 12px;color:darkred;'>" & rs.Fields(x).Name &
"</th><td  style='font-family:Calibri,  Sans-Serif;font-size: 12px;color:navy;'>" &
rs.Fields(x).Value & "</td></tr>"""")")
            Case "Button"
            txtstream.WriteLine      ("document.WriteLn(""""<tr><th      style='font-
family:Calibri, Sans-Serif;font-size: 12px;color:darkred;'>" & rs.Fields(x).Name &
"</th><td style='font-family:Calibri, Sans-Serif;font-size: 12px;color:navy;'><input
type=button Value='" & rs.Fields(x).Value & "'></input></td></tr>"""")")
            Case "Combobox"
            txtstream.WriteLine      ("document.WriteLn(""""<tr><th      style='font-
family:Calibri, Sans-Serif;font-size: 12px;color:darkred;'>" & rs.Fields(x).Name &
"</th>        <td       style='font-family:Calibri,      Sans-Serif;font-size:
12px;color:navy;'><select><option   Value='"   &   rs.Fields(x).Value   &   "'>"   &
rs.Fields(x).Value & "</option></select></td></tr>"""")")
            Case "Div"
            txtstream.WriteLine      ("document.WriteLn(""""<tr><th      style='font-
family:Calibri, Sans-Serif;font-size: 12px;color:darkred;'>" & rs.Fields(x).Name &
"</th><td style='font-family:Calibri, Sans-Serif;font-size: 12px;color:navy;'><div>"
& rs.Fields(x).Value & "</div></td></tr>"""")")
            Case "Listbox"
            txtstream.WriteLine      ("document.WriteLn(""""<tr><th      style='font-
family:Calibri, Sans-Serif;font-size: 12px;color:darkred;'>" & rs.Fields(x).Name &
"</th><td style='font-family:Calibri, Sans-Serif;font-size: 12px;color:navy;'><select
multiple=true><option Value ='" & rs.Fields(x).Value & "'>" & rs.Fields(x).Value &
"</option></select></td></tr>"""")")
            Case "Span"
            txtstream.WriteLine      ("document.WriteLn(""""<tr><th      style='font-
family:Calibri, Sans-Serif;font-size: 12px;color:darkred;'>" & rs.Fields(x).Name &
"</th><td        style='font-family:Calibri,        Sans-Serif;font-size:
12px;color:navy;'><span>" & rs.Fields(x).Value & "</span></td></tr>"""")")
            Case "Textbox"
            txtstream.WriteLine      ("document.WriteLn(""""<tr><th      style='font-
family:Calibri, Sans-Serif;font-size: 12px;color:darkred;'>" & rs.Fields(x).Name &
"</th><td style='font-family:Calibri, Sans-Serif;font-size: 12px;color:navy;'><input
type=text Value='" & rs.Fields(x).Value & "'></input></td></tr>"""")")
            Case "Textarea"
            txtstream.WriteLine      ("document.WriteLn(""""<tr><th      style='font-
family:Calibri, Sans-Serif;font-size: 12px;color:darkred;'>" & rs.Fields(x).Name &
```

```
                 "</th><td          style='font-family:Calibri,          Sans-Serif;font-size:
12px;color:navy;'><textarea>" & rs.Fields(x).Value & "</textarea></td></tr>""")")

                End Select

           Next


           Case "Multi-Line Vertical"


              Select Case TableType

                 Case "Table"

                    txtstream.WriteLine  ("document.WriteLn(""<table  Border='1'
cellpadding='1' cellspacing='1'>"")")

                 Case "Report"

                    txtstream.WriteLine  ("document.WriteLn(""<table  Border='0'
cellpadding='1' cellspacing='1'>"")")

              End Select


              For x = 0 To rs.Fields.Count - 1

                    txtstream.WriteLine  ("document.WriteLn(""<tr><th  style='font-
family:Calibri, Sans-Serif;font-size: 12px;color:darkred;'>" & rs.Fields(x).Name &
"</th>"")")

              rs.MoveFirst

              Do While rs.EOF = False


                 Select Case ControlType

                    Case "None"
```

```
                    txtstream.WriteLine        ("document.WriteLn(""<td        style='font-
family:Calibri,   Sans-Serif;font-size:   12px;color:navy;'>" & rs.Fields(x).Value   &
"</td>"")")
                            Case "Button"
                    txtstream.WriteLine        ("document.WriteLn(""<td        style='font-
family:Calibri, Sans-Serif;font-size: 12px;color:navy;'><input type=button Value='"
& rs.Fields(x).Value & "'></input></td>"")")
                            Case "Combobox"
                    txtstream.WriteLine        ("document.WriteLn(""<td        style='font-
family:Calibri, Sans-Serif;font-size: 12px;color:navy;'><select><option Value='" &
rs.Fields(x).Value & "'>" & rs.Fields(x).Value & "</option></select></td>"")")
                            Case "Div"
                    txtstream.WriteLine        ("document.WriteLn(""<td        style='font-
family:Calibri, Sans-Serif;font-size: 12px;color:navy;'><div>" & rs.Fields(x).Value &
"</div></td>"")")
                            Case "Listbox"
                    txtstream.WriteLine        ("document.WriteLn(""<td        style='font-
family:Calibri,          Sans-Serif;font-size:          12px;color:navy;'><select
multiple=true><option Value ='" & rs.Fields(x).Value & "'>" & rs.Fields(x).Value &
"</option></select></td>"")")
                            Case "Span"
                    txtstream.WriteLine        ("document.WriteLn(""<td        style='font-
family:Calibri, Sans-Serif;font-size: 12px;color:navy;'><span>" & rs.Fields(x).Value
& "</span></td>"")")
                            Case "Textbox"
                    txtstream.WriteLine        ("document.WriteLn(""<td        style='font-
family:Calibri, Sans-Serif;font-size: 12px;color:navy;'><input type=text Value='" &
rs.Fields(x).Value & "'></input></td>"")")
                            Case "Textarea"
                    txtstream.WriteLine        ("document.WriteLn(""<td        style='font-
family:Calibri,       Sans-Serif;font-size:       12px;color:navy;'><textarea>"       &
rs.Fields(x).Value & "</textarea></td>"")")

                    End Select

                    rs.MoveNext

                Loop

                txtstream.WriteLine ("document.WriteLn(""</tr>"")")
```

```vb
                Next

            End Select


        Else

            Select Case Orientation

                Case "Single-Line Horizontal"

                Select Case TableType

                Case "Table"

                    txtstream.WriteLine   ("document.WriteLn(""<table  Border='1'
cellpadding='1' cellspacing='1' datasrc=#rs>"")")

                Case "Report"

                    txtstream.WriteLine   ("document.WriteLn(""<table  Border='0'
cellpadding='1' cellspacing='1' datasrc=#rs>"")")

                End Select


                txtstream.WriteLine ("document.WriteLn(""<tr>"")")
                For x = 0 To rs.Fields.Count - 1

                    txtstream.WriteLine          ("document.WriteLn(""<th>"      &
rs.Fields(x).Name & "</th>"")")

                Next
                txtstream.WriteLine ("document.WriteLn(""</tr>"")")
                txtstream.WriteLine ("document.WriteLn(""<tr>"")")
```

```vb
For x = 0 To rs.Fields.Count - 1


    Select Case ControlType

        Case "None"
        txtstream.WriteLine ("document.WriteLn(""<td>" & rs.Fields(x).Value
& "</td>"")")
        Case "Button"
        txtstream.WriteLine ("document.WriteLn(""<td><input  type=button
Value='" & rs.Fields(x).Value & "'></input></td>"")")
        Case "Combobox"
        txtstream.WriteLine       ("document.WriteLn(""<td><select><option
Value='"   &   rs.Fields(x).Value   &   "'>"   &   rs.Fields(x).Value   &
"</option></select></td>"")")
        Case "Div"
        txtstream.WriteLine       ("document.WriteLn(""<td><div>"       &
rs.Fields(x).Value & "</div></td>"")")
        Case "Listbox"
        txtstream.WriteLine              ("document.WriteLn(""<td><select
multiple=true><option Value ='" & rs.Fields(x).Value & "'>" & rs.Fields(x).Value &
"</option></select></td>"")")
        Case "Span"
        txtstream.WriteLine       ("document.WriteLn(""<td><span>"       &
rs.Fields(x).Value & "</span></td>"")")
        Case "Textbox"
        txtstream.WriteLine     ("document.WriteLn(""<td><input     type=text
Value='" & rs.Fields(x).Value & "'></input></td>"")")
        Case "Textarea"
        txtstream.WriteLine     ("document.WriteLn(""<td><textarea>"      &
rs.Fields(x).Value & "</textarea></td>"")")

    End Select


Next

txtstream.WriteLine ("document.WriteLn(""</tr>"")")
```

```vb
Case "Multi-Line Horizontal"

    Select Case TableType

        Case "Table"

            txtstream.WriteLine ("document.WriteLn(""<table Border='1' cellpadding='1' cellspacing='1'>"")")

        Case "Report"

            txtstream.WriteLine ("document.WriteLn(""<table Border='0' cellpadding='1' cellspacing='1'>"")")

    End Select

    txtstream.WriteLine ("document.WriteLn(""<tr>"")")
    For x = 0 To rs.Fields.Count - 1

        txtstream.WriteLine ("document.WriteLn(""<th>" & rs.Fields(x).Name & "</th>"")")

    Next
    txtstream.WriteLine ("document.WriteLn(""</tr>"")")
    Do While rs.EOF = False

        txtstream.WriteLine ("document.WriteLn(""<tr>"")")
        For x = 0 To rs.Fields.Count - 1

            Select Case ControlType

                Case "None"
                txtstream.WriteLine ("document.WriteLn(""<td>" & rs.Fields(x).Value & "</td>"")")
                Case "Button"
                txtstream.WriteLine ("document.WriteLn(""<td><input type=button Value='" & rs.Fields(x).Value & "'></input></td>"")")
                Case "Combobox"
```

```
                    txtstream.WriteLine        ("document.WriteLn(""""<td><select><option
Value='"      &      rs.Fields(x).Value      &      "'>"      &      rs.Fields(x).Value      &
"</option></select></td>""")")
                              Case "Div"
                    txtstream.WriteLine        ("document.WriteLn(""""<td><div>"          &
rs.Fields(x).Value & "</div></td>""")")
                              Case "Listbox"
                    txtstream.WriteLine              ("document.WriteLn(""""<td><select
multiple=true><option Value ='" & rs.Fields(x).Value & "'>" & rs.Fields(x).Value &
"</option></select></td>""")")
                              Case "Span"
                    txtstream.WriteLine        ("document.WriteLn(""""<td><span>"        &
rs.Fields(x).Value & "</span></td>""")")
                              Case "Textbox"
                    txtstream.WriteLine   ("document.WriteLn(""""<td><input   type=text
Value='" & rs.Fields(x).Value & "'></input></td>""")")
                              Case "Textarea"
                    txtstream.WriteLine        ("document.WriteLn(""""<td><textarea>"      &
rs.Fields(x).Value & "</textarea></td>""")")


             End Select


         Next
         txtstream.WriteLine ("document.WriteLn(""""</tr>""")")
         rs.MoveNext
      Loop



      Case "Single-Line Vertical"


      Select Case TableType

      Case "Table"

             txtstream.WriteLine   ("document.WriteLn(""""<table   Border='1'
cellpadding='1' cellspacing='1'>""")")
```

```vb
            Case "Report"

                    txtstream.WriteLine  ("document.WriteLn(""""<table  Border='0'
cellpadding='1' cellspacing='1'>"""")")

        End Select

        For x = 0 To rs.Fields.Count - 1

            Select Case ControlType

                Case "None"
                    txtstream.WriteLine          ("document.WriteLn(""""<tr><th>"          &
rs.Fields(x).Name & "</th><td>" & rs.Fields(x).Value & "</td></tr>"""")")
                Case "Button"
                    txtstream.WriteLine          ("document.WriteLn(""""<tr><th>"          &
rs.Fields(x).Name & "</th><td><input type=button Value='" & rs.Fields(x).Value &
"'></input></td></tr>"""")")
                Case "Combobox"
                    txtstream.WriteLine          ("document.WriteLn(""""<tr><th>"          &
rs.Fields(x).Name & "</th> <td><select><option Value='" & rs.Fields(x).Value &
"'>" & rs.Fields(x).Value & "</option></select></td></tr>"""")")
                Case "Div"
                    txtstream.WriteLine          ("document.WriteLn(""""<tr><th>"          &
rs.Fields(x).Name       &        "</th><td><div>"       &        rs.Fields(x).Value       &
"</div></td></tr>"""")")
                Case "Listbox"
                    txtstream.WriteLine          ("document.WriteLn(""""<tr><th>"          &
rs.Fields(x).Name  &  "</th><td><select  multiple=true><option  Value  ='"  &
rs.Fields(x).Value & "'>" & rs.Fields(x).Value & "</option></select></td></tr>"""")")
                Case "Span"
                    txtstream.WriteLine          ("document.WriteLn(""""<tr><th>"          &
rs.Fields(x).Name       &        "</th><td><span>"       &        rs.Fields(x).Value       &
"</span></td></tr>"""")")
                Case "Textbox"
                    txtstream.WriteLine          ("document.WriteLn(""""<tr><th>"          &
rs.Fields(x).Name & "</th><td><input type=text Value='" & rs.Fields(x).Value &
"'></input></td></tr>"""")")
                Case "Textarea"
```

```
                    txtstream.WriteLine        ("document.WriteLn(""<tr><th>"        &
rs.Fields(x).Name        &        "</th><td><textarea>"        &        rs.Fields(x).Value        &
"</textarea></td></tr>"")")

            End Select

        Next


        Case "Multi-Line Vertical"


            Select Case TableType

            Case "Table"

                    txtstream.WriteLine        ("document.WriteLn(""<table    Border='1'
cellpadding='1' cellspacing='1'>"")")

                Case "Report"

                    txtstream.WriteLine        ("document.WriteLn(""<table    Border='0'
cellpadding='1' cellspacing='1'>"")")

            End Select


            For x = 0 To rs.Fields.Count - 1

                    txtstream.WriteLine        ("document.WriteLn(""<tr><th>"        &
rs.Fields(x).Name & "</th>"")")

                rs.MoveFirst

                Do While rs.EOF = False


                    Select Case ControlType

                    Case "None"
```

```vb
            txtstream.WriteLine                    ("document.WriteLn(""<td>"          &
rs.Fields(x).Value & "</td>"")")
                        Case "Button"
            txtstream.WriteLine ("document.WriteLn(""<td><input type=button
Value='" & rs.Fields(x).Value & "'></input></td>"")")
                        Case "Combobox"
            txtstream.WriteLine        ("document.WriteLn(""<td><select><option
Value='"      &      rs.Fields(x).Value      &      "'>"      &      rs.Fields(x).Value      &
"</option></select></td>"")")
                        Case "Div"
            txtstream.WriteLine                    ("document.WriteLn(""<td><div>"        &
rs.Fields(x).Value & "</div></td>"")")
                        Case "Listbox"
            txtstream.WriteLine                       ("document.WriteLn(""<td><select
multiple=true><option Value ='" & rs.Fields(x).Value & "'>" & rs.Fields(x).Value &
"</option></select></td>"")")
                        Case "Span"
            txtstream.WriteLine          ("document.WriteLn(""<td><span>"         &
rs.Fields(x).Value & "</span></td>"")")
                        Case "Textbox"
            txtstream.WriteLine    ("document.WriteLn(""<td><input    type=text
Value='" & rs.Fields(x).Value & "'></input></td>"")")
                        Case "Textarea"
            txtstream.WriteLine          ("document.WriteLn(""<td><textarea>"        &
rs.Fields(x).Value & "</textarea></td>"")")

                End Select

                rs.MoveNext

        Loop

        txtstream.WriteLine ("document.WriteLn(""</tr>"")")

    Next


    End Select
```

```
        End If

        txtstream.WriteLine ("document.WriteLn("""</table>""")")
        txtstream.WriteLine (Chr(60) & "/script>")
        txtstream.WriteLine ("</body>")
        txtstream.WriteLine ("</html>")
        txtstream.Close


        tempstr = ""
        Set txtstream = fso.OpenTextFile(ws.CurrentDirectory & "\" & Tablename &
".html", 1, True, -2)
        Do While txtstream.AtEndOfStream = False
           tempstr = tempstr & txtstream.ReadLine()
           tempstr = tempstr & vbCrLf
        Loop
        txtstream.Close
        textarea1.innerText = tempstr

    End Sub

    Sub Do_Cloaked()


       Select Case EngineConfiguration


          Case "cncmdrs"


                Set cn = CreateObject("ADODB.Connection")
                Set cmd = CreateObject("ADODB.Command")
                Set rs = CreateObject("ADODB.Recordset")


                cn.ConnectionString = "Provider=" & Provider & ";Data Source=" &
fName.Value & ";"
                Call cn.Open()

                cmd.ActiveConnection = cn
```

```
            cmd.CommandType = 8
            cmd.CommandText = strQuery
            Call cmd.Execute()

            rs.CursorLocation = 3
            rs.LockType = 3
            Call rs.Open(cmd)


    Case "cnrs"

            Set cn = CreateObject("ADODB.Connection")
            Set rs = CreateObject("ADODB.Recordset")

            cn.ConnectionString = "Provider=" & Provider & ";Data Source=" &
fName.Value & ";"
            Call cn.Open()

            rs.ActiveConnection = cn
            rs.CursorLocation = 3
            rs.LockType = 3
            rs.Source = strQuery
            Call rs.Open()

    Case "cmdrs"

            Set cmd = CreateObject("ADODB.Command")
            Set rs = CreateObject("ADODB.Recordset")

            cmd.ActiveConnection = "Provider=" & Provider & ";Data Source=" &
fName.Value & ";"
            cmd.CommandType = 8
            cmd.CommandText = strQuery
            Call cmd.Execute()

            rs.CursorLocation = 3
            rs.LockType = 3
            Call rs.Open(cmd)

    Case "rs"
```

```
        Set rs = CreateObject("ADODB.Recordset")
        rs.ActiveConnection = "Provider=" & Provider & ";Data Source=" &
fName.Value & ";"
        rs.LockType = 3
        rs.Cursorlocation = 3
        rs.Source = strQuery
        Call rs.Open()

    End Select


        Set ws = CreateObject("WScript.Shell")
        Set fso = CreateObject("Scripting.FileSystemObject")

        Set txtstream = fso.OpenTextFile(ws.CurrentDirectory & "\" & Tablename &
".html", 2, True, -2)
        txtstream.WriteLine ("<html>")
        txtstream.WriteLine ("<head>")
        txtstream.WriteLine ("<title>" & Tablename & "</title>")

    Add_The_StyleSheet

        txtstream.WriteLine ("</head>")
        txtstream.WriteLine ("<body>")
        txtstream.WriteLine ("<script language='vbscript'>")
        txtstream.WriteLine ("")
        txtstream.WriteLine ("dim mystr")
        txtstream.WriteLine ("")
        txtstream.WriteLine ("Sub Window_OnLoad()")
        txtstream.WriteLine ("")

    If StyleSheet = "InLine" Then


        Select Case Orientation


            Case "Single-Line Horizontal"
```

```
Select Case TableType

    Case "Table"

        txtstream.WriteLine ("mystr = mystr & ""<table Border='1'
cellpadding='1' cellspacing='1' datasrc=#rs>""" & vbcrlf")

    Case "Report"

        txtstream.WriteLine ("mystr = mystr & ""<table Border='0'
cellpadding='1' cellspacing='1' datasrc=#rs>""" & vbcrlf")

    End Select


    txtstream.WriteLine ("mystr = mystr & ""<tr>""" & vbcrlf")
    For x = 0 To rs.Fields.Count - 1

        txtstream.WriteLine ("mystr = mystr & ""<th style='font-
family:Calibri, Sans-Serif;font-size: 12px;color:darkred;'>" & rs.Fields(x).Name &
"</th>""" & vbcrlf")

    Next
    txtstream.WriteLine ("mystr = mystr & ""</tr>""" & vbcrlf")
    txtstream.WriteLine ("mystr = mystr & ""<tr>""" & vbcrlf")
    For x = 0 To rs.Fields.Count - 1


    Select Case ControlType

        Case "None"
    txtstream.WriteLine ("mystr = mystr & ""<td style='font-
family:Calibri, Sans-Serif;font-size: 12px;color:navy;'>" & rs.Fields(x).Value &
"</td>""" & vbcrlf")
        Case "Button"
    txtstream.WriteLine ("mystr = mystr & ""<td style='font-
family:Calibri, Sans-Serif;font-size: 12px;color:navy;'><input type=button Value='"
& rs.Fields(x).Value & "'></input></td>""" & vbcrlf")
        Case "Combobox"
```

```
                  txtstream.WriteLine ("mystr = mystr & ""<td style='font-
family:Calibri, Sans-Serif;font-size: 12px;color:navy;'><select><option Value='" &
rs.Fields(x).Value & "'>" & rs.Fields(x).Value & "</option></select></td>""" &
vbcrlf")
                        Case "Div"
                  txtstream.WriteLine ("mystr = mystr & ""<td style='font-
family:Calibri, Sans-Serif;font-size: 12px;color:navy;'><div>" & rs.Fields(x).Value &
"</div></td>""" & vbcrlf")
                        Case "Listbox"
                  txtstream.WriteLine ("mystr = mystr & ""<td style='font-
family:Calibri,          Sans-Serif;font-size:          12px;color:navy;'><select
multiple=true><option Value ='" & rs.Fields(x).Value & "'>" & rs.Fields(x).Value &
"</option></select></td>""" & vbcrlf")
                        Case "Span"
                  txtstream.WriteLine ("mystr = mystr & ""<td style='font-
family:Calibri, Sans-Serif;font-size: 12px;color:navy;'><span>" & rs.Fields(x).Value
& "</span></td>""" & vbcrlf")
                        Case "Textbox"
                  txtstream.WriteLine ("mystr = mystr & ""<td style='font-
family:Calibri, Sans-Serif;font-size: 12px;color:navy;'><input type=text Value='" &
rs.Fields(x).Value & "'></input></td>""" & vbcrlf")
                        Case "Textarea"
                  txtstream.WriteLine ("mystr = mystr & ""<td style='font-
family:Calibri,          Sans-Serif;font-size:          12px;color:navy;'><textarea>"      &
rs.Fields(x).Value & "</textarea></td>""" & vbcrlf")

                  End Select



                  Next

                  txtstream.WriteLine ("mystr = mystr & ""</tr>""" & vbcrlf")



            Case "Multi-Line Horizontal"



                  Select Case TableType
```

```
            Case "Table"

                    txtstream.WriteLine ("mystr = mystr & """<table Border='1'
cellpadding='1' cellspacing='1'>""" & vbcrlf")

            Case "Report"

                    txtstream.WriteLine ("mystr = mystr & """<table Border='0'
cellpadding='1' cellspacing='1'>""" & vbcrlf")

        End Select

        txtstream.WriteLine ("mystr = mystr & """<tr>""" & vbcrlf")
        For x = 0 To rs.Fields.Count - 1

                    txtstream.WriteLine ("mystr = mystr & """<th style='font-
family:Calibri, Sans-Serif;font-size: 12px;color:darkred;'>" & rs.Fields(x).Name &
"</th>""" & vbcrlf")

        Next
        txtstream.WriteLine ("mystr = mystr & """</tr>""" & vbcrlf")
        Do While rs.EOF = False

        txtstream.WriteLine ("mystr = mystr & """<tr>""" & vbcrlf")
        For x = 0 To rs.Fields.Count - 1

            Select Case ControlType

                Case "None"
        txtstream.WriteLine ("mystr = mystr & """<td style='font-
family:Calibri, Sans-Serif;font-size: 12px;color:navy;'>" & rs.Fields(x).Value &
"</td>""" & vbcrlf")
                Case "Button"
        txtstream.WriteLine ("mystr = mystr & """<td style='font-
family:Calibri, Sans-Serif;font-size: 12px;color:navy;'><input type=button Value='"
& rs.Fields(x).Value & "'></input></td>""" & vbcrlf")
                Case "Combobox"
        txtstream.WriteLine ("mystr = mystr & """<td style='font-
family:Calibri, Sans-Serif;font-size: 12px;color:navy;'><select><option Value='" &
```

rs.Fields(x).Value & "'>" & rs.Fields(x).Value & "</option></select></td>"" & vbcrlf")
                        Case "Div"
            txtstream.WriteLine ("mystr = mystr & ""<td style='font-family:Calibri, Sans-Serif;font-size: 12px;color:navy;'> " & rs.Fields(x).Value & " </td>"" & vbcrlf")
                        Case "Listbox"
            txtstream.WriteLine ("mystr = mystr & ""<td style='font-family:Calibri,   Sans-Serif;font-size: 12px;color:navy;'><select multiple=true><option Value ='" & rs.Fields(x).Value & "'>" & rs.Fields(x).Value & "</option></select></td>"" & vbcrlf")
                        Case "Span"
            txtstream.WriteLine ("mystr = mystr & ""<td style='font-family:Calibri, Sans-Serif;font-size: 12px;color:navy;'>" & rs.Fields(x).Value & "</td>"" & vbcrlf")
                        Case "Textbox"
            txtstream.WriteLine ("mystr = mystr & ""<td style='font-family:Calibri, Sans-Serif;font-size: 12px;color:navy;'><input type=text Value='" & rs.Fields(x).Value & "'></input></td>"" & vbcrlf")
                        Case "Textarea"
            txtstream.WriteLine ("mystr = mystr & ""<td style='font-family:Calibri,   Sans-Serif;font-size: 12px;color:navy;'><textarea>"   & rs.Fields(x).Value & "</textarea></td>"" & vbcrlf")

            End Select

        Next
        txtstream.WriteLine ("mystr = mystr & ""</tr>"" & vbcrlf")
        rs.MoveNext
    Loop

    Case "Single-Line Vertical"

    Select Case TableType

        Case "Table"

```
            txtstream.WriteLine ("mystr = mystr & ""<table Border='1'
cellpadding='1' cellspacing='1'>"" & vbcrlf")

        Case "Report"

            txtstream.WriteLine ("mystr = mystr & ""<table Border='0'
cellpadding='1' cellspacing='1'>"" & vbcrlf")

        End Select

        For x = 0 To rs.Fields.Count - 1

        Select Case ControlType

            Case "None"
            txtstream.WriteLine ("mystr = mystr & ""<tr><th style='font-
family:Calibri, Sans-Serif;font-size: 12px;color:darkred;'>" & rs.Fields(x).Name &
"</th><td style='font-family:Calibri, Sans-Serif;font-size: 12px;color:navy;'>" &
rs.Fields(x).Value & "</td></tr>"" & vbcrlf")
            Case "Button"
            txtstream.WriteLine ("mystr = mystr & ""<tr><th style='font-
family:Calibri, Sans-Serif;font-size: 12px;color:darkred;'>" & rs.Fields(x).Name &
"</th><td style='font-family:Calibri, Sans-Serif;font-size: 12px;color:navy;'><input
type=button Value='" & rs.Fields(x).Value & "'></input></td></tr>"" & vbcrlf")
            Case "Combobox"
            txtstream.WriteLine ("mystr = mystr & ""<tr><th style='font-
family:Calibri, Sans-Serif;font-size: 12px;color:darkred;'>" & rs.Fields(x).Name &
"</th>        <td        style='font-family:Calibri,        Sans-Serif;font-size:
12px;color:navy;'><select><option  Value='"  &  rs.Fields(x).Value  &  "'>"  &
rs.Fields(x).Value & "</option></select></td></tr>"" & vbcrlf")
            Case "Div"
            txtstream.WriteLine ("mystr = mystr & ""<tr><th style='font-
family:Calibri, Sans-Serif;font-size: 12px;color:darkred;'>" & rs.Fields(x).Name &
"</th><td style='font-family:Calibri, Sans-Serif;font-size: 12px;color:navy;'><div>"
& rs.Fields(x).Value & "</div></td></tr>"" & vbcrlf")
            Case "Listbox"
            txtstream.WriteLine ("mystr = mystr & ""<tr><th style='font-
family:Calibri, Sans-Serif;font-size: 12px;color:darkred;'>" & rs.Fields(x).Name &
"</th><td style='font-family:Calibri, Sans-Serif;font-size: 12px;color:navy;'><select
```

```
multiple=true><option Value ='" & rs.Fields(x).Value & "'>" & rs.Fields(x).Value &
"</option></select></td></tr>"" & vbcrlf")
                    Case "Span"
            txtstream.WriteLine ("mystr = mystr & ""<tr><th style='font-
family:Calibri, Sans-Serif;font-size: 12px;color:darkred;'>" & rs.Fields(x).Name &
"</th><td          style='font-family:Calibri,          Sans-Serif;font-size:
12px;color:navy;'><span>" & rs.Fields(x).Value & "</span></td></tr>"" & vbcrlf")
                    Case "Textbox"
            txtstream.WriteLine ("mystr = mystr & ""<tr><th style='font-
family:Calibri, Sans-Serif;font-size: 12px;color:darkred;'>" & rs.Fields(x).Name &
"</th><td style='font-family:Calibri, Sans-Serif;font-size: 12px;color:navy;'><input
type=text Value='" & rs.Fields(x).Value & "'></input></td></tr>"" & vbcrlf")
                    Case "Textarea"
            txtstream.WriteLine ("mystr = mystr & ""<tr><th style='font-
family:Calibri, Sans-Serif;font-size: 12px;color:darkred;'>" & rs.Fields(x).Name &
"</th><td          style='font-family:Calibri,          Sans-Serif;font-size:
12px;color:navy;'><textarea>" & rs.Fields(x).Value & "</textarea></td></tr>"" &
vbcrlf")


            End Select

        Next


        Case "Multi-Line Vertical"


        Select Case TableType

            Case "Table"

                txtstream.WriteLine ("mystr = mystr & ""<table Border='1'
cellpadding='1' cellspacing='1'>"" & vbcrlf")

            Case "Report"

                txtstream.WriteLine ("mystr = mystr & ""<table Border='0'
cellpadding='1' cellspacing='1'>"" & vbcrlf")

        End Select
```

```vb
For x = 0 To rs.Fields.Count - 1

        txtstream.WriteLine ("mystr = mystr & ""<tr><th style='font-
family:Calibri, Sans-Serif;font-size: 12px;color:darkred;'>" & rs.Fields(x).Name &
"</th>""" & vbcrlf")

    rs.MoveFirst

    Do While rs.EOF = False


        Select Case ControlType

            Case "None"
        txtstream.WriteLine ("mystr = mystr & ""<td style='font-
family:Calibri, Sans-Serif;font-size: 12px;color:navy;'>" & rs.Fields(x).Value &
"</td>""" & vbcrlf")
            Case "Button"
        txtstream.WriteLine ("mystr = mystr & ""<td style='font-
family:Calibri, Sans-Serif;font-size: 12px;color:navy;'><input type=button Value='"
& rs.Fields(x).Value & "'></input></td>""" & vbcrlf")
            Case "Combobox"
        txtstream.WriteLine ("mystr = mystr & ""<td style='font-
family:Calibri, Sans-Serif;font-size: 12px;color:navy;'><select><option Value='" &
rs.Fields(x).Value & "'>" & rs.Fields(x).Value & "</option></select></td>""" &
vbcrlf")
            Case "Div"
        txtstream.WriteLine ("mystr = mystr & ""<td style='font-
family:Calibri, Sans-Serif;font-size: 12px;color:navy;'><div>" & rs.Fields(x).Value &
"</div></td>""" & vbcrlf")
            Case "Listbox"
        txtstream.WriteLine ("mystr = mystr & ""<td style='font-
family:Calibri,            Sans-Serif;font-size:           12px;color:navy;'><select
multiple=true><option Value ='" & rs.Fields(x).Value & "'>" & rs.Fields(x).Value &
"</option></select></td>""" & vbcrlf")
            Case "Span"
```

```
                    txtstream.WriteLine ("mystr = mystr & ""<td style='font-
family:Calibri, Sans-Serif;font-size: 12px;color:navy;'><span>" & rs.Fields(x).Value
& "</span></td>"" & vbcrlf")
                        Case "Textbox"
                    txtstream.WriteLine ("mystr = mystr & ""<td style='font-
family:Calibri, Sans-Serif;font-size: 12px;color:navy;'><input type=text Value='" &
rs.Fields(x).Value & "'></input></td>"" & vbcrlf")
                        Case "Textarea"
                    txtstream.WriteLine ("mystr = mystr & ""<td style='font-
family:Calibri,      Sans-Serif;font-size:      12px;color:navy;'><textarea>"      &
rs.Fields(x).Value & "</textarea></td>"" & vbcrlf")

                    End Select

                    rs.MoveNext

                Loop

                txtstream.WriteLine ("mystr = mystr & ""</tr>"" & vbcrlf")

            Next

        End Select



    Else


        Select Case Orientation


            Case "Single-Line Horizontal"

                Select Case TableType

                    Case "Table"
```

```
                    txtstream.WriteLine ("mystr = mystr & ""<table Border='1'
cellpadding='1' cellspacing='1' datasrc=#rs>"" & vbcrlf")

            Case "Report"

                    txtstream.WriteLine ("mystr = mystr & ""<table Border='0'
cellpadding='1' cellspacing='1' datasrc=#rs>"" & vbcrlf")

            End Select


        txtstream.WriteLine ("mystr = mystr & ""<tr>"" & vbcrlf")
        For x = 0 To rs.Fields.Count - 1

                txtstream.WriteLine     ("mystr    =    mystr    &    ""<th>"   &
rs.Fields(x).Name & "</th>"" & vbcrlf")

        Next
        txtstream.WriteLine ("mystr = mystr & ""</tr>"" & vbcrlf")
        txtstream.WriteLine ("mystr = mystr & ""<tr>"" & vbcrlf")
        For x = 0 To rs.Fields.Count - 1


            Select Case ControlType

                Case "None"
            txtstream.WriteLine ("mystr = mystr & ""<td>" & rs.Fields(x).Value &
"</td>"" & vbcrlf")
                Case "Button"
            txtstream.WriteLine ("mystr = mystr & ""<td><input type=button
Value='" & rs.Fields(x).Value & "'></input></td>"" & vbcrlf")
                Case "Combobox"
            txtstream.WriteLine ("mystr   =   mystr   &   ""<td><select><option
Value='"    &    rs.Fields(x).Value   &    "'>"   &    rs.Fields(x).Value   &
"</option></select></td>"" & vbcrlf")
                Case "Div"
            txtstream.WriteLine ("mystr   =   mystr   &   ""<td><div>"   &
rs.Fields(x).Value & "</div></td>"" & vbcrlf")
                Case "Listbox"
```

```vb
            txtstream.WriteLine    ("mystr    =    mystr    &    ""<td><select
multiple=true><option Value ='" & rs.Fields(x).Value & "'>" & rs.Fields(x).Value &
"</option></select></td>""" & vbcrlf")
                    Case "Span"
            txtstream.WriteLine    ("mystr    =    mystr    &    ""<td><span>"    &
rs.Fields(x).Value & "</span></td>""" & vbcrlf")
                    Case "Textbox"
            txtstream.WriteLine    ("mystr    =    mystr    &    ""<td><input    type=text
Value='" & rs.Fields(x).Value & "'></input></td>""" & vbcrlf")
                    Case "Textarea"
            txtstream.WriteLine    ("mystr    =    mystr    &    ""<td><textarea>"    &
rs.Fields(x).Value & "</textarea></td>""" & vbcrlf")

            End Select


                    Next

            txtstream.WriteLine ("mystr = mystr & ""</tr>""" & vbcrlf")


            Case "Multi-Line Horizontal"


            Select Case TableType

                Case "Table"

                    txtstream.WriteLine    ("mystr    =    mystr    &    ""<table    Border='1'
cellpadding='1' cellspacing='1'>""" & vbcrlf")

                Case "Report"

                    txtstream.WriteLine    ("mystr    =    mystr    &    ""<table    Border='0'
cellpadding='1' cellspacing='1'>""" & vbcrlf")

            End Select

            txtstream.WriteLine ("mystr = mystr & ""<tr>""" & vbcrlf")
```

```vb
            For x = 0 To rs.Fields.Count - 1

                    txtstream.WriteLine    ("mystr   =   mystr   &   """<th>"   &
rs.Fields(x).Name & "</th>""" & vbcrlf")

            Next
            txtstream.WriteLine ("mystr = mystr & """</tr>""" & vbcrlf")
            Do While rs.EOF = False

                txtstream.WriteLine ("mystr = mystr & """<tr>""" & vbcrlf")
                For x = 0 To rs.Fields.Count - 1

                Select Case ControlType

                    Case "None"
                    txtstream.WriteLine ("mystr = mystr & """<td>" & rs.Fields(x).Value
& "</td>""" & vbcrlf")
                        Case "Button"
                    txtstream.WriteLine ("mystr = mystr & """<td><input type=button
Value='" & rs.Fields(x).Value & "'></input></td>""" & vbcrlf")
                        Case "Combobox"
                    txtstream.WriteLine    ("mystr   =   mystr   &   """<td><select><option
Value='"     &     rs.Fields(x).Value     &     "'>"     &     rs.Fields(x).Value     &
"</option></select></td>""" & vbcrlf")
                        Case "Div"
                    txtstream.WriteLine    ("mystr   =   mystr   &   """<td><div>"   &
rs.Fields(x).Value & "</div></td>""" & vbcrlf")
                        Case "Listbox"
                    txtstream.WriteLine    ("mystr   =   mystr   &   """<td><select
multiple=true><option Value ='" & rs.Fields(x).Value & "'>" & rs.Fields(x).Value &
"</option></select></td>""" & vbcrlf")
                        Case "Span"
                    txtstream.WriteLine    ("mystr   =   mystr   &   """<td><span>"   &
rs.Fields(x).Value & "</span></td>""" & vbcrlf")
                        Case "Textbox"
                    txtstream.WriteLine ("mystr = mystr & """<td><input type=text
Value='" & rs.Fields(x).Value & "'></input></td>""" & vbcrlf")
                        Case "Textarea"
                    txtstream.WriteLine ("mystr = mystr & """<td><textarea>" &
rs.Fields(x).Value & "</textarea></td>""" & vbcrlf")
```

```
            End Select


        Next
        txtstream.WriteLine ("mystr = mystr & """"</tr>"""" & vbcrlf")
        rs.MoveNext
    Loop



Case "Single-Line Vertical"


    Select Case TableType

        Case "Table"

            txtstream.WriteLine ("mystr = mystr & """"<table Border='1'
cellpadding='1' cellspacing='1'>"""" & vbcrlf")

        Case "Report"

            txtstream.WriteLine ("mystr = mystr & """"<table Border='0'
cellpadding='1' cellspacing='1'>"""" & vbcrlf")

    End Select

    For x = 0 To rs.Fields.Count - 1

        Select Case ControlType

            Case "None"
            txtstream.WriteLine ("mystr = mystr & """"<tr><th>" &
rs.Fields(x).Name & "</th><td>" & rs.Fields(x).Value & "</td></tr>"""" & vbcrlf")
            Case "Button"
            txtstream.WriteLine ("mystr = mystr & """"<tr><th>" &
rs.Fields(x).Name & "</th><td><input type=button Value='" & rs.Fields(x).Value &
"'></input></td></tr>"""" & vbcrlf")
            Case "Combobox"
```

```vb
            txtstream.WriteLine    ("mystr    =    mystr    &    ""<tr><th>"    &
rs.Fields(x).Name & "</th> <td><select><option Value='" & rs.Fields(x).Value &
"'>" & rs.Fields(x).Value & "</option></select></td></tr>""" & vbcrlf")
            Case "Div"
            txtstream.WriteLine    ("mystr    =    mystr    &    ""<tr><th>"    &
rs.Fields(x).Name & "</th><td><div>" & rs.Fields(x).Value & "</div></td></tr>""" &
vbcrlf")
            Case "Listbox"
            txtstream.WriteLine    ("mystr    =    mystr    &    ""<tr><th>"    &
rs.Fields(x).Name  &  "</th><td><select  multiple=true><option  Value ='"  &
rs.Fields(x).Value & "'>" & rs.Fields(x).Value & "</option></select></td></tr>""" &
vbcrlf")
            Case "Span"
            txtstream.WriteLine    ("mystr    =    mystr    &    ""<tr><th>"    &
rs.Fields(x).Name    &    "</th><td><span>"    &    rs.Fields(x).Value    &
"</span></td></tr>""" & vbcrlf")
            Case "Textbox"
            txtstream.WriteLine    ("mystr    =    mystr    &    ""<tr><th>"    &
rs.Fields(x).Name & "</th><td><input type=text Value='" & rs.Fields(x).Value &
"'></input></td></tr>""" & vbcrlf")
            Case "Textarea"
            txtstream.WriteLine    ("mystr    =    mystr    &    ""<tr><th>"    &
rs.Fields(x).Name    &    "</th><td><textarea>"    &    rs.Fields(x).Value    &
"</textarea></td></tr>""" & vbcrlf")

        End Select

    Next


    Case "Multi-Line Vertical"


    Select Case TableType

    Case "Table"

        txtstream.WriteLine ("mystr = mystr & ""<table Border='1'
cellpadding='1' cellspacing='1'>""" & vbcrlf")
```

```vb
        Case "Report"

                txtstream.WriteLine ("mystr = mystr & """"<table Border='0'
cellpadding='1' cellspacing='1'>"""" & vbcrlf")

        End Select


        For x = 0 To rs.Fields.Count - 1

                txtstream.WriteLine ("mystr    =    mystr   &   """"<tr><th>"   &
rs.Fields(x).Name & "</th>"""" & vbcrlf")

        rs.MoveFirst

        Do While rs.EOF = False


        Select Case ControlType

                Case "None"
                txtstream.WriteLine ("mystr = mystr & """"<td>" & rs.Fields(x).Value
& "</td>"""" & vbcrlf")
                Case "Button"
                txtstream.WriteLine ("mystr = mystr & """"<td><input type=button
Value='" & rs.Fields(x).Value & "'></input></td>"""" & vbcrlf")
                Case "Combobox"
                txtstream.WriteLine ("mystr  =  mystr  &  """"<td><select><option
Value='"   &   rs.Fields(x).Value   &   "'>"   &   rs.Fields(x).Value   &
"</option></select></td>"""" & vbcrlf")
                Case "Div"
                txtstream.WriteLine ("mystr   =   mystr   &   """"<td><div>"   &
rs.Fields(x).Value & "</div></td>"""" & vbcrlf")
                Case "Listbox"
                txtstream.WriteLine ("mystr    =    mystr    &    """"<td><select
multiple=true><option Value ='" & rs.Fields(x).Value & "'>" & rs.Fields(x).Value &
"</option></select></td>"""" & vbcrlf")
                Case "Span"
                txtstream.WriteLine ("mystr   =   mystr   &   """"<td><span>"   &
rs.Fields(x).Value & "</span></td>"""" & vbcrlf")
```

```
                    Case "Textbox"
                    txtstream.WriteLine ("mystr = mystr & ""<td><input type=text
Value='" & rs.Fields(x).Value & "'></input></td>""" & vbcrlf")
                    Case "Textarea"
                    txtstream.WriteLine ("mystr = mystr & ""<td><textarea>" &
rs.Fields(x).Value & "</textarea></td>""" & vbcrlf")

               End Select

               rs.MoveNext

          Loop

               txtstream.WriteLine ("mystr = mystr & ""</tr>""" & vbcrlf")

          Next

     End Select


     End If

     txtstream.WriteLine ("mystr = mystr & ""</table>""" & vbcrlf")
     txtstream.WriteLine ("document.WriteLn(mystr)")
     txtstream.WriteLine ("")
     txtstream.WriteLine ("End Sub")
     txtstream.WriteLine ("")
     txtstream.WriteLine (Chr(60) & "/script>")
     txtstream.WriteLine ("</body>")
     txtstream.WriteLine ("</html>")
     txtstream.Close



     tempstr = ""
     Set txtstream = fso.OpenTextFile(ws.CurrentDirectory & "\" & Tablename &
".html", 1, True, -2)
     Do While txtstream.AtEndOfStream = False
          tempstr = tempstr & txtstream.ReadLine()
```

```
            tempstr = tempstr & vbCrLf
        Loop
        txtstream.Close
        textarea1.innerText = tempstr

    End Sub

    Sub Do__Bound()

        Select Case EngineConfiguration


            Case "cncmdrs"


                Set cn = CreateObject("ADODB.Connection")
                Set cmd = CreateObject("ADODB.Command")
                Set rs = CreateObject("ADODB.Recordset")


                cn.ConnectionString = "Provider=" & provider & ";Data Source=" &
fName.Value & ";"
                Call cn.Open()

                cmd.ActiveConnection = cn
                cmd.CommandType = 8
                cmd.CommandText = strQuery
                Call cmd.Execute()

                rs.CursorLocation = 3
                rs.LockType = 3
                Call rs.Open(cmd)


            Case "cnrs"

                Set cn = CreateObject("ADODB.Connection")
                Set rs = CreateObject("ADODB.Recordset")
```

```vb
            cn.ConnectionString = "Provider=" & Provider & ";Data Source=" &
fName.Value & ";"
            Call cn.Open()

            rs.ActiveConnection = cn
            rs.CursorLocation = 3
            rs.LockType = 3
            rs.Source = strQuery
            Call rs.Open()

        Case "cmdrs"

            Set cmd = CreateObject("ADODB.Command")
            Set rs = CreateObject("ADODB.Recordset")

            cmd.ActiveConnection = "Provider=" & Provider & ";Data Source=" &
fName.Value & ";"
            cmd.CommandType = 8
            cmd.CommandText = strQuery
            Call cmd.Execute()

            rs.CursorLocation = 3
            rs.LockType = 3
            Call rs.Open(cmd)

        Case "rs"

        Set rs = CreateObject("ADODB.Recordset")
        rs.ActiveConnection = "Provider=" & Provider & ";Data Source=" &
fName.Value & ";"
            rs.LockType = 3
            rs.Cursorlocation = 3
            rs.Source = strQuery
            Call rs.Open()

    End Select

        Set ws = CreateObject("WScript.Shell")
        Set fso = CreateObject("Scripting.FileSystemObject")
```

```
        Set txtstream = fso.OpenTextFile(ws.CurrentDirectory & "\" & Tablename &
".html", 2, True, -2)
        txtstream.WriteLine ("<html>")
        txtstream.WriteLine ("<head>")
        txtstream.WriteLine ("<title>" & Tablename & "</title>")


    Add_The_StyleSheet


    Select Case HTMLEngineConfiguration


      Case "cncmdrs"


        txtstream.WriteLine  ("<object  id=""cmd""  CLASSID=""clsid:00000507-
0000-0010-8000-00AA006D2EA4"" height=""0"" width=""0""></object>")
        txtstream.WriteLine  ("<object  id=""cn""     CLASSID=""clsid:00000514-
0000-0010-8000-00AA006D2EA4"" height=""0"" width=""0""></object>")
        txtstream.WriteLine  ("<object  id=""rs""     CLASSID=""clsid:00000535-
0000-0010-8000-00AA006D2EA4"" height=""0"" width=""0""></object>")
        txtstream.WriteLine ("</head>")
        txtstream.WriteLine ("<body>")
        txtstream.WriteLine ("<script language='vbscript'>")
        txtstream.WriteLine ("")
        txtstream.WriteLine ("cn.ConnectionString = ""Provider=" & Provider &
";Data Source=" & fName.Value & ";"" ")
        txtstream.WriteLine ("Call cn.Open()")
        txtstream.WriteLine ("")
        txtstream.WriteLine ("cmd.ActiveConnection = cn")
        txtstream.WriteLine ("cmd.CommandType = 8")
        txtstream.WriteLine ("cmd.CommandText = """ & strQuery & """ ")
        txtstream.WriteLine ("Call cmd.Execute()")
        txtstream.WriteLine ("")
        txtstream.WriteLine ("rs.CursorLocation = 3")
        txtstream.WriteLine ("rs.LockType = 3")
        txtstream.WriteLine ("Call rs.Open(cmd)")
        txtstream.WriteLine ("")
        txtstream.WriteLine (Chr(60) & "/script>")
```

```
Case "cnrs"

        txtstream.WriteLine ("<object id=""cn"" CLASSID=""clsid:00000514-0000-
0010-8000-00AA006D2EA4"" height=""0"" width=""0""></object>")
        txtstream.WriteLine ("<object id=""rs"" CLASSID=""clsid:00000535-0000-
0010-8000-00AA006D2EA4"" height=""0"" width=""0""></object>")
        txtstream.WriteLine ("</head>")
        txtstream.WriteLine ("<body>")
        txtstream.WriteLine ("<script language='vbscript'>")
        txtstream.WriteLine ("")
        txtstream.WriteLine ("cn.ConnectionString = ""Provider=" & Provider &
";Data Source=" & fName.Value & ";"" ")
        txtstream.WriteLine ("Call cn.Open()")
        txtstream.WriteLine ("")
        txtstream.WriteLine ("rs.ActiveConnection = cn")
        txtstream.WriteLine ("rs.CursorLocation = 3")
        txtstream.WriteLine ("rs.LockType = 3")
        txtstream.WriteLine ("rs.Source = """ & strQuery & """ ")
        txtstream.WriteLine ("Call rs.Open()")
        txtstream.WriteLine ("")
        txtstream.WriteLine (Chr(60) & "/script>")


    Case "cmdrs"

        txtstream.WriteLine ("<object id=""cmd"" CLASSID=""clsid:00000507-
0000-0010-8000-00AA006D2EA4"" height=""0"" width=""0""></object>")
        txtstream.WriteLine ("<object id=""rs"" CLASSID=""clsid:00000535-
0000-0010-8000-00AA006D2EA4"" height=""0"" width=""0""></object>")
        txtstream.WriteLine ("</head>")
        txtstream.WriteLine ("<body>")
        txtstream.WriteLine ("<script language='vbscript'>")
        txtstream.WriteLine ("")
        txtstream.WriteLine ("cmd.ActiveConnection = ""Provider=" & Provider &
";Data Source=" & fName.Value & ";"" ")
        txtstream.WriteLine ("cmd.CommandType = 8")
        txtstream.WriteLine ("cmd.CommandText = """ & strQuery & """ ")
        txtstream.WriteLine ("Call cmd.Execute()")
```

```
txtstream.WriteLine ("")
txtstream.WriteLine ("rs.CursorLocation = 3")
txtstream.WriteLine ("rs.LockType = 3")
txtstream.WriteLine ("Call rs.Open(cmd)")
txtstream.WriteLine ("")
txtstream.WriteLine (Chr(60) & "/script>")

    Case "rs"



        txtstream.WriteLine ("<object id=""rs"" CLASSID=""clsid:00000535-0000-
0010-8000-00AA006D2EA4"" height=""0"" width=""0""></object>")
        txtstream.WriteLine ("</head>")
        txtstream.WriteLine ("<body>")
        txtstream.WriteLine ("<script language='vbscript'>")
        txtstream.WriteLine ("")
        txtstream.WriteLine ("rs.ActiveConnection = ""Provider=" & Provider &
";Data Source=" & fName.Value & ";"" ")
        txtstream.WriteLine ("rs.LockType = 3")
        txtstream.WriteLine ("rs.Cursorlocation = 3")
        txtstream.WriteLine ("rs.Source = """ & strQuery & """ ")
        txtstream.WriteLine ("Call rs.Open()")
        txtstream.WriteLine ("")
        txtstream.WriteLine (Chr(60) & "/script>")

    End Select


    If StyleSheet = "InLine" Then


        Select Case Orientation


            Case "Single-Line Horizontal"

                Select Case TableType

                    Case "Table"
```

```
                txtstream.WriteLine    ("<table    Border='1'    cellpadding='1'
cellspacing='1'>")

        Case "Report"

                txtstream.WriteLine    ("<table    Border='0'    cellpadding='1'
cellspacing='1'>")

        End Select


        txtstream.WriteLine ("<tr>")
        For x = 0 To rs.Fields.Count - 1

                txtstream.WriteLine    ("<th    style='font-family:Calibri,    Sans-
Serif;font-size: 12px;color:darkred;'>" & rs.Fields(x).Name & "</th>")

        Next
        txtstream.WriteLine ("</tr>")
        txtstream.WriteLine ("<tr>")
        For x = 0 To rs.Fields.Count - 1

        Select Case ControlType

            Case "Button"
        txtstream.WriteLine ("<td style='font-family:Calibri, Sans-Serif;font-
size:    12px;color:navy;'><input    type=button    datasrc=#rs    datafld='"    &
rs.Fields(x).Name & "'></input></td>")
            Case "Combobox"
        txtstream.WriteLine ("<td style='font-family:Calibri, Sans-Serif;font-
size: 12px;color:navy;'><select datasrc=#rs datafld='" & rs.Fields(x).Name &
"'></select></td>")
            Case "Div"
        txtstream.WriteLine ("<td style='font-family:Calibri, Sans-Serif;font-
size:  12px;color:navy;'><div  datasrc=#rs  datafld='"  &  rs.Fields(x).Name  &
"'></div></td>")
            Case "Listbox"
```

```
            txtstream.WriteLine ("<td style='font-family:Calibri, Sans-Serif;font-
size:  12px;color:navy;'><select   multiple=true   datasrc=#rs   datafld='"   &
rs.Fields(x).Name & "'></option></select></td>")
            Case "Span"
            txtstream.WriteLine ("<td style='font-family:Calibri, Sans-Serif;font-
size:  12px;color:navy;'><span  datasrc=#rs  datafld='"  &  rs.Fields(x).Name  &
"'></span></td>")
            Case "Textbox"
            txtstream.WriteLine ("<td style='font-family:Calibri, Sans-Serif;font-
size: 12px;color:navy;'><input type=text datasrc=#rs datafld='" & rs.Fields(x).Name
& "'></input></td>")
            Case "Textarea"
            txtstream.WriteLine ("<td style='font-family:Calibri, Sans-Serif;font-
size: 12px;color:navy;'><textarea datasrc=#rs datafld='"  &  rs.Fields(x).Name  &
"'></textarea></td>")

        End Select

    Next

    txtstream.WriteLine ("</tr>")


Case "Multi-Line Horizontal"


    Select Case TableType

    Case "Table"

            txtstream.WriteLine     ("<table     Border='1'     cellpadding='1'
cellspacing='1' datasrc=#rs>")

    Case "Report"

            txtstream.WriteLine     ("<table     Border='0'     cellpadding='1'
cellspacing='1' datasrc=#rs>")

    End Select
```

```
txtstream.WriteLine ("<thead><tr>")
For x = 0 To rs.Fields.Count - 1


        txtstream.WriteLine    ("<th    style='font-family:Calibri,    Sans-
Serif;font-size: 12px;color:darkred;'>" & rs.Fields(x).Name & "</th>")


    Next
    txtstream.WriteLine ("</tr></thead>")
    txtstream.WriteLine ("<tbody><tr>")
    For x = 0 To rs.Fields.Count - 1

    Select Case ControlType

        Case "Button"
        txtstream.WriteLine ("<td style='font-family:Calibri, Sans-Serif;font-
size:    12px;color:navy;'><input    type=button    datasrc=#rs    datafld='"    &
rs.Fields(x).Name & "'></input></td>")
        Case "Combobox"
        txtstream.WriteLine ("<td style='font-family:Calibri, Sans-Serif;font-
size:  12px;color:navy;'><select  datasrc=#rs  datafld='"  &  rs.Fields(x).Name  &
"'></select></td>")
        Case "Div"
        txtstream.WriteLine ("<td style='font-family:Calibri, Sans-Serif;font-
size:  12px;color:navy;'><div  datasrc=#rs  datafld='"  &  rs.Fields(x).Name  &
"'></div></td>")
        Case "Listbox"
        txtstream.WriteLine ("<td style='font-family:Calibri, Sans-Serif;font-
size:    12px;color:navy;'><select    multiple=true    datasrc=#rs    datafld='"    &
rs.Fields(x).Name & "'></option></select></td>")
        Case "Span"
        txtstream.WriteLine ("<td style='font-family:Calibri, Sans-Serif;font-
size:  12px;color:navy;'><span  datasrc=#rs  datafld='"  &  rs.Fields(x).Name  &
"'></span></td>")
        Case "Textbox"
        txtstream.WriteLine ("<td style='font-family:Calibri, Sans-Serif;font-
size: 12px;color:navy;'><input type=text datasrc=#rs datafld='" & rs.Fields(x).Name
& "'></input></td>")
        Case "Textarea"
```

```vb
            txtstream.WriteLine ("<td style='font-family:Calibri, Sans-Serif;font-
size: 12px;color:navy;'><textarea datasrc=#rs datafld='" & rs.Fields(x).Name &
"'></textarea></td>")

        End Select

    Next

        txtstream.WriteLine ("</tr></tbody>")



    Case "Single-Line Vertical"

        Select Case TableType

        Case "Table"

                txtstream.WriteLine      ("<table    Border='1'    cellpadding='1'
cellspacing='1'>")

            Case "Report"

                txtstream.WriteLine      ("<table    Border='0'    cellpadding='1'
cellspacing='1'>")

        End Select

        For x = 0 To rs.Fields.Count - 1

        Select Case ControlType

            Case "Button"
            txtstream.WriteLine ("<td style='font-family:Calibri, Sans-Serif;font-
size:   12px;color:navy;'><input    type=button   datasrc=#rs   datafld='"     &
rs.Fields(x).Name & "'></input></td>")
                Case "Combobox"
```

```
            txtstream.WriteLine ("<td style='font-family:Calibri, Sans-Serif;font-
size: 12px;color:navy;'><select datasrc=#rs datafld='" & rs.Fields(x).Name &
"'></select></td>")
                    Case "Div"
            txtstream.WriteLine ("<td style='font-family:Calibri, Sans-Serif;font-
size: 12px;color:navy;'><div datasrc=#rs datafld='" & rs.Fields(x).Name &
"'></div></td>")
                    Case "Listbox"
            txtstream.WriteLine ("<td style='font-family:Calibri, Sans-Serif;font-
size: 12px;color:navy;'><select multiple=true datasrc=#rs datafld='" &
rs.Fields(x).Name & "'></option></select></td>")
                    Case "Span"
            txtstream.WriteLine ("<td style='font-family:Calibri, Sans-Serif;font-
size: 12px;color:navy;'><span datasrc=#rs datafld='" & rs.Fields(x).Name &
"'></span></td>")
                    Case "Textbox"
            txtstream.WriteLine ("<td style='font-family:Calibri, Sans-Serif;font-
size: 12px;color:navy;'><input type=text datasrc=#rs datafld='" & rs.Fields(x).Name
& "'></input></td>")
                    Case "Textarea"
            txtstream.WriteLine ("<td style='font-family:Calibri, Sans-Serif;font-
size: 12px;color:navy;'><textarea datasrc=#rs datafld='" & rs.Fields(x).Name &
"'></textarea></td>")


                End Select

            Next


        End Select

    Else

    Select Case Orientation


        Case "Single-Line Horizontal"

        Select Case TableType
```

```
                Case "Table"

                        txtstream.WriteLine      ("<table     Border='1'    cellpadding='1'
cellspacing='1'>")

                Case "Report"

                        txtstream.WriteLine      ("<table     Border='0'    cellpadding='1'
cellspacing='1'>")

        End Select


        txtstream.WriteLine ("<tr>")
        For x = 0 To rs.Fields.Count - 1

            txtstream.WriteLine ("<th >" & rs.Fields(x).Name & "</th>")

        Next
        txtstream.WriteLine ("</tr>")
        txtstream.WriteLine ("<tr>")
        For x = 0 To rs.Fields.Count - 1

        Select Case ControlType

                Case "Button"
                txtstream.WriteLine ("<td ><input type=button datasrc=#rs datafld='"
& rs.Fields(x).Name & "'></input></td>")
                Case "Combobox"
                txtstream.WriteLine   ("<td   ><select   datasrc=#rs   datafld='"   &
rs.Fields(x).Name & "'></select></td>")
                Case "Div"
                txtstream.WriteLine   ("<td   ><div   datasrc=#rs   datafld='"   &
rs.Fields(x).Name & "'></div></td>")
                Case "Listbox"
                txtstream.WriteLine   ("<td   ><select   multiple=true   datasrc=#rs
datafld='" & rs.Fields(x).Name & "'></option></select></td>")
                Case "Span"
                txtstream.WriteLine   ("<td   ><span   datasrc=#rs   datafld='"   &
rs.Fields(x).Name & "'></span></td>")
```

```vb
                Case "Textbox"
            txtstream.WriteLine ("<td ><input type=text datasrc=#rs datafld='" &
rs.Fields(x).Name & "'></input></td>")
                Case "Textarea"
            txtstream.WriteLine ("<td ><textarea datasrc=#rs datafld='" &
rs.Fields(x).Name & "'></textarea></td>")

            End Select



        Next

        txtstream.WriteLine ("</tr>")


    Case "Multi-Line Horizontal"


        Select Case TableType

            Case "Table"

                txtstream.WriteLine ("<table Border='1' cellpadding='1'
cellspacing='1' datasrc=#rs>")

            Case "Report"

                txtstream.WriteLine ("<table Border='0' cellpadding='1'
cellspacing='1' datasrc=#rs>")

        End Select

        txtstream.WriteLine ("<thead><tr>")
        For x = 0 To rs.Fields.Count - 1

            txtstream.WriteLine ("<th >" & rs.Fields(x).Name & "</th>")

        Next
        txtstream.WriteLine ("</tr></thead>")
```

```
txtstream.WriteLine ("<tbody><tr>")
For x = 0 To rs.Fields.Count - 1

    Select Case ControlType

        Case "Button"
    txtstream.WriteLine ("<td ><input type=button datasrc=#rs datafld='"
& rs.Fields(x).Name & "'></input></td>")
        Case "Combobox"
    txtstream.WriteLine ("<td    ><select    datasrc=#rs    datafld='"    &
rs.Fields(x).Name & "'></select></td>")
        Case "Div"
    txtstream.WriteLine ("<td    ><div    datasrc=#rs    datafld='"    &
rs.Fields(x).Name & "'></div></td>")
        Case "Listbox"
    txtstream.WriteLine ("<td    ><select    multiple=true    datasrc=#rs
datafld='" & rs.Fields(x).Name & "'></option></select></td>")
        Case "Span"
    txtstream.WriteLine ("<td    ><span    datasrc=#rs    datafld='"    &
rs.Fields(x).Name & "'></span></td>")
        Case "Textbox"
    txtstream.WriteLine ("<td ><input type=text datasrc=#rs datafld='" &
rs.Fields(x).Name & "'></input></td>")
        Case "Textarea"
    txtstream.WriteLine ("<td    ><textarea    datasrc=#rs    datafld='"    &
rs.Fields(x).Name & "'></textarea></td>")

    End Select

Next

    txtstream.WriteLine ("</tr></tbody>")



Case "Single-Line Vertical"


    Select Case TableType
```

```
                Case "Table"

                        txtstream.WriteLine    ("<table    Border='1'    cellpadding='1'
cellspacing='1'>")

                Case "Report"

                        txtstream.WriteLine    ("<table    Border='0'    cellpadding='1'
cellspacing='1'>")

        End Select

        For x = 0 To rs.Fields.Count - 1

        Select Case ControlType

                Case "Button"
                txtstream.WriteLine ("<td ><input type=button datasrc=#rs datafld='"
& rs.Fields(x).Name & "'></input></td>")
                Case "Combobox"
                txtstream.WriteLine    ("<td    ><select    datasrc=#rs    datafld='"    &
rs.Fields(x).Name & "'></select></td>")
                Case "Div"
                txtstream.WriteLine    ("<td    ><div    datasrc=#rs    datafld='"    &
rs.Fields(x).Name & "'></div></td>")
                Case "Listbox"
                txtstream.WriteLine    ("<td    ><select    multiple=true    datasrc=#rs
datafld='" & rs.Fields(x).Name & "'></option></select></td>")
                Case "Span"
                txtstream.WriteLine    ("<td    ><span    datasrc=#rs    datafld='"    &
rs.Fields(x).Name & "'></span></td>")
                Case "Textbox"
                txtstream.WriteLine ("<td ><input type=text datasrc=#rs datafld='" &
rs.Fields(x).Name & "'></input></td>")
                Case "Textarea"
                txtstream.WriteLine    ("<td    ><textarea    datasrc=#rs    datafld='"    &
rs.Fields(x).Name & "'></textarea></td>")

        End Select
```

```
            Next

        End Select


    End If

        txtstream.WriteLine ("</table>")
        txtstream.WriteLine ("</body>")
        txtstream.WriteLine ("</html>")
        txtstream.Close



        tempstr = ""
        Set txtstream = fso.OpenTextFile(ws.CurrentDirectory & "\" & Tablename &
".html", 1, True, -2)
        Do While txtstream.AtEndOfStream = False
            tempstr = tempstr & txtstream.ReadLine()
            tempstr = tempstr & vbCrLf
        Loop
        txtstream.Close
        textarea1.innerText = tempstr


    End Sub

    Sub LT1_OnClick()

        If fName.Value = "" then
            msgbox("Please provide the location and name of the database you want to
use before clicking here.")
            exit sub
        else
            cnstr = "Provider=" & Provider & ";Data Source = " & FName.Value & ";"

            Set cn = CreateObject("ADODB.Connection")
```

```
On Error Resume Next
cn.ConnectionString = cnstr
Call cn.Open()
if err.number = 0 then
    Set ws = CreateObject("WScript.Shell")
    Set fso = CreateObject("Scripting.FileSystemObject")
    Set txtstream = fso.OpenTextFile(ws.CurrentDirectory & "\tables.txt", 2,
true, -2)
    Set rs1 = cn.OpenSchema(20)
    Dim l()
    Redim l(3)
    l(0) = Len("Tablename")
    l(1) = Len("TableType")
    l(2) = Len("Description")

    Do While rs1.EOF = false
        if len(rs1.Fields("TABLE_NAME").Value) > l(0) then
            l(0) = len(rs1.Fields("TABLE_NAME").Value)
        End If

        if len(rs1.Fields("TABLE_TYPE").Value) > l(1) then
            l(1) = len(rs1.Fields("TABLE_TYPE").Value)
        End If

        if len(rs1.Fields("TABLE_DESCRIPTION").Value) > l(2) then
            l(2) = len(rs1.Fields("TABLE_DESCRIPTION").Value)
        End If

        rs1.MoveNext
    Loop

    rs1.MoveFirst

    l(0) = l(0) + 3
    l(1) = l(1) + 3
    l(2) = l(2) + 3

    Dim v

    v = l(0) - Len("Tablename")
```

```
mystr = "Tablename" & space(v)
v = l(1) - Len("TableType")
mystr = mystr & "TableType" & space(v)
v = l(2) - Len("Description")
mystr = mystr & "Description" & space(v)
txtstream.WriteLine(mystr)
mystr = ""
txtstream.WriteLine("")

Set tbl = document.GetElementByID("trex")
tbl.innerHTML = ""
Set opt = document.createElement("option")
opt.value = "*Select An Option*"
opt.text = "*Select An Option*"
opt.Selected = true
tbl.Options.Add(opt)



Do While rs1.EOF = false



    If mid(rs1.Fields("TABLE_NAME").Value, 1,4) <> "MSys" then

        If rs1.Fields("TABLE_TYPE").Value = "TABLE" then
            Set opt = document.createElement("option")
            opt.value = rs1.Fields("TABLE_NAME").Value
            opt.text = rs1.Fields("TABLE_NAME").Value
            tbl.Options.Add(opt)
        End If

                v = l(0) - Len(rs1.Fields("TABLE_NAME").Value)
                mystr = rs1.Fields("TABLE_NAME").Value & space(v)
                v = l(1) - Len(rs1.Fields("TABLE_TYPE").Value)
                mystr = mystr & rs1.Fields("TABLE_TYPE").Value & space(v)
                v = l(2) - Len(rs1.Fields("DESCRIPTION").Value)
                mystr = mystr & rs1.Fields("DESCRIPTION").Value
                txtstream.WriteLine(mystr)
                mystr = ""
```

```
            End If
            rs1.MoveNext
        Loop

        Dim tempstr
        tempstr = ""
        Set txtstream = fso.OpenTextFile(ws.CurrentDirectory & "\tables.txt", 1,
true, -2)
        Do While txtstream.AtEndOfStream = false
            tempstr = tempstr & txtstream.ReadLine()
            tempstr = tempstr & vbcrlf
        loop
        txtstream.Close
        textarea1.innerText = tempstr
    Else

        msgbox("Test connection Failed with: " & err.Description)

    End IF

    End If

    strQuery = ""

End Sub

Sub TestConnection1_OnClick()

    If fName.Value = "" then
        msgbox("Please provide the location and name of the database you want to
use before clicking here.")
        exit sub
    else
        cnstr = "Provider=" & Provider & ";Data Source = " & FName.Value & ";"
        Set cn = CreateObject("ADODB.Connection")
        On Error Resume Next
        cn.ConnectionString = cnstr
        Call cn.Open()
        if err.number = 0 then
            msgbox("Test connection succeeded.")
```

```vbscript
        else
           msgbox("Connecion failed with: " & err.Description)
        End If
      End If


    End Sub


    Sub Search_OnClick()


      Set ws = CreateObject("WScript.Shell")
      Set OpenDialog1 = CreateObject("MSComDlg.CommonDialog")


      With OpenDialog1
        .DialogTitle = "Open Database"
        .InitDir = ws.CurrentDirectory
        .Filter = "Microsoft Older Access Database(*.mdb)|*.mdb|Microsoft Newer
Access Database(*.accdb)|*.accdb"
        .FilterIndex = 2
        .MaxFileSize =32000
        .Flags = 2621952
        .ShowOpen
      End With
      If OpenDialog1.Filename <> "" then
         FName.Value = OpenDialog1.Filename
      End If


    End Sub


    Sub DataLinks1_OnClick()


    Set cn = createObject("ADODB.Connection")
    Set dl = CreateObject("Datalinks")
    Set cn = dl.PromptNew()
    Provider= cn.Provider
    cnstr = cn.ConnectionString
    FName.Value = cn.Properties("Data Source").Value


    End Sub


    Sub Clipboard1_OnClick()
```

```vbs
        Set range = Textarea1.createTextRange()
        call range.findText(Textarea1.InnerText)
        range.select
        Call document.execCommand("Copy")
        Call document.execCommand("Unselect")


    End Sub

    Sub RunMe_OnClick()

        Set ws = CreateObject("WScript.Shell")
        Set fso = CreateObject("Scripting.FileSystemObject")

        Set txtstream = fso.OpenTextFile(ws.CurrentDirectory & "\" & Tablename &
".vbs", 2, true, -2)
        txtstream.WriteLine(Textarea1.innerText)
        txtstream.Close()
        Set txtstream = nothing
        Dim shorty
        Shorty = fso.GetFolder(ws.CurrentDirectory).ShortPath
        call ws.Run("C:\Windows\SysWOW64\wscript.exe " & Shorty & "\Code.vbs")
        Set fso = nothing

    End Sub

    Sub ViewMe_OnClick()

        Set ws = CreateObject("WScript.Shell")
        Set fso = CreateObject("Scripting.FileSystemObject")
        Dim shorty
        Shorty = fso.GetFolder(ws.CurrentDirectory).ShortPath
        Set txtstream = fso.OpenTextFile(shorty & "\" & Tablename & ".hta", 2, true, -
2)
        txtstream.WriteLine(Textarea1.innerText)
        txtstream.Close()
        call ws.Run(Shorty & "\" & Tablename & ".hta")
        Set fso = nothing
        Set ws = nothing
```

```vb
End Sub

Sub Document_OnClick()

End Sub

Sub wd_OnClick()

    Dim oWord
    Set range = Textarea1.createTextRange()
    Call range.findText(Textarea1.InnerText)
    range.Select
    Call Document.execCommand("Copy")
    Set oWordApp = CreateObject("Word.Application")
    oWordApp.Visible = True
    oWordApp.Activate
    Set oWord = oWordApp.Documents.Add()
    Set oParagraph = oWord.Application.ActiveDocument.Paragraphs.Add()
    oParagraph.Alignment = wdAlignParagraphJustify
    oParagraph.range.Font.Name = "Merriweather"
    oParagraph.range.Font.Size = 8
    oParagraph.CharacterUnitFirstLineIndent = 0.3
    oParagraph.Format.LineSpacing = 1.5
    oParagraph.Format.LineUnitBefore = 0
    oParagraph.Format.LineUnitAfter = 0
    oParagraph.range.PasteAndFormat (22)
    Call Document.execCommand("Unselect")

End Sub

Sub EMail_OnClick()

    if sn.Value = "" Then
        msgbox("Please enter the name of the mail server you want to connect to
before clicking here.")
        Exit Sub
    End If

    if lnu.Value = "" Then
```

```
        msgbox("Please enter your Logon name you use to log into mail server to
before clicking here.")
        Exit Sub
        End If

    if lpwd.Value = "" Then
        msgbox("Please enter your Logon password you use to log into mail server to
before clicking here.")
        Exit Sub
        End If

    if emfn.Value = "" Then
        msgbox("Please enter the user friendly name you use send and receive mail
before clicking here.")
        Exit Sub
        End If

    if ema.Value = "" Then
        msgbox("Please enter your email address you use send and receive mail before
clicking here.")
        Exit Sub
        End If

    if rec.Value = "" Then
        msgbox("Please enter the email address of the person you want to send this
mail to before clicking here.")
        Exit Sub
        End If

    if s.Value = "" Then
        msgbox("Please enter a subject or title you want to use with this mail before
clicking here.")
        Exit Sub
        End If


    Dim SMTPServer
    Dim SMTPLogon
    Dim LogonUserName
    Dim LogonPassword
```

```vbscript
Dim strHTML
Dim shorty
Set ws = CreateObject("WScript.Shell")
Set fso = CreateObject("Scripting.FileSystemObject")
Shorty = fso.GetFolder(ws.CurrentDirectory).ShortPath
Set txtstream = fso.OpenTextFile(shorty & "\" & Tablename & ".hta", 1, true, -
2)
Do While txtstream.AtEndOfStream = false
  strHTML = strHTML & txtstream.ReadLine()
  strHTML = strHTML & vbcrlf
Loop
txtstream.Close()

EMailFrom = ema.Value
EmailFromName = emfn.Value
EmailTo = rec.Value
SMTPServer = sn.Value
SMTPLogon = lnu.Value
SMTPPassword = lpwd.Value




Const SMTPSSL = True
Const SMTPPort = 465

Const cdoSendUsingPickup = 1   'Send message using local SMTP service pickup
directory.
Const cdoSendUsingPort = 2     'Send the message using SMTP over TCP/IP
networking.

Const cdoAnonymous = 0      ' No authentication
Const cdoBasic = 1      ' BASIC clear text authentication
Const cdoNTLM = 2      ' NTLM, Microsoft proprietary authentication

' First, create the message

Set objMessage = CreateObject("CDO.Message")
objMessage.Subject = s.Value
objMessage.From = """" & EmailFromName & """" <" & EmailFrom & ">"
```

```
objMessage.To = EmailTo
objMessage.HTMLBody = strHTML

' Second, configure the server

objMessage.Configuration.Fields.Item("http://schemas.microsoft.com/cdo/config
uration/sendusing") = 2
objMessage.Configuration.Fields.Item("http://schemas.microsoft.com/cdo/config
uration/smtpusessl") = true
objMessage.Configuration.Fields.Item("http://schemas.microsoft.com/cdo/config
uration/smtpserver") = SMTPServer
objMessage.Configuration.Fields.Item("http://schemas.microsoft.com/cdo/config
uration/smtpauthenticate") = cdoBasic
objMessage.Configuration.Fields.Item("http://schemas.microsoft.com/cdo/config
uration/sendusername") = SMTPLogon
objMessage.Configuration.Fields.Item("http://schemas.microsoft.com/cdo/config
uration/sendpassword") = SMTPPassword
objMessage.Configuration.Fields.Item("http://schemas.microsoft.com/cdo/config
uration/smtpserverport") = SMTPPort
objMessage.Configuration.Fields.Item("http://schemas.microsoft.com/cdo/config
uration/smtpconnectiontimeout") = 60
Call objMessage.Configuration.Fields.Update()

On Error Resume Next

Call objMessage.Send()

If err.Number = 0 then

    Msgbox("Your message has been sent successfully!")

else

    Msgbox("Unable to send the mail. Error Message: " & err.Description)

    err.Clear

End If

End Sub
```

```
Sub Providers_OnClick()

    Const HKEY_LOCAL_MACHINE = &H80000002
    strComputer = "."
    Dim strValue
    Set                         oReg                         =
GetObject("winmgmts:{impersonationLevel=impersonate}!\\.\root\default:StdRegPr
ov")
    oReg.EnumKey                            HKEY_LOCAL_MACHINE,
"SOFTWARE\Wow6432Node\Classes\CLSID", SubKeyNames
    mystr       =           "Providers       found        in
HKEY_LOCAL_MACHINE\SOFTWARE\Wow6432Node\Classes\CLSID" & vbCrLf
    For Each skn In SubKeyNames
        If                oReg.GetStringValue(HKEY_LOCAL_MACHINE,
"SOFTWARE\Wow6432Node\Classes\CLSID\" & skn & "\Ole Db Provider", "",
strValue) = 0 Then
            oReg.GetStringValue             HKEY_LOCAL_MACHINE,
"SOFTWARE\Wow6432Node\Classes\CLSID\" & skn, "", strValue
        mystr = mystr & strValue & vbCrLf
        End If
    Next
    mystr = mystr & "" & vbCrLf
    Textarea1.innerText = mystr

End Sub

Sub Drivers_OnClick()

    const HKEY_LOCAL_MACHINE = &H80000002
    strComputer = "."
    Set                                              oReg=
GetObject("winmgmts:{impersonationLevel=impersonate}!\\.\root\default:StdRegPr
ov")

    if          oReg.EnumValues          (HKEY_LOCAL_MACHINE,
"SOFTWARE\Wow6432Node\ODBC\ODBCINST.INI\ODBC Drivers", SubKeyNames) =
0 Then
```

```
        mystr           =           "Drivers         found        in
HKEY_LOCAL_MACHINE\SOFTWARE\Wow6432Node\ODBC\ODBCINST.INI\ODBC
Drivers" & vbcrlf
        mystr = mystr & "" & vbcrlf
        for each skn in SubKeyNames
            mystr = mystr & skn & vbcrlf
        Next
        mystr = mystr & "" & vbcrlf
        Textarea1.innerText = mystr
    End If

    End Sub

    Sub ISAMS_OnClick()

    Dim tempstr
    Dim SubKeyNames

    const HKEY_LOCAL_MACHINE = &H80000002
    strComputer = "."
    Set                                                       oreg=
GetObject("winmgmts:{impersonationLevel=impersonate}!\\.\root\default:StdRegPr
ov")
        if                        oreg.EnumKey(HKEY_LOCAL_MACHINE,
    "SOFTWARE\Wow6432Node\Microsoft\Jet 3.5\ISAM Formats", SubKeyNames) = 0
then
        mystr       =       "Found      Jet      3.5      ISAMS      in
HKEY_LOCAL_MACHINE\Wow6432Node\Microsoft\Jet 3.5\ISAM Formats" & vbcrlf
        mystr = mystr & "" & vbcrlf
        for each skn in SubKeyNames
            mystr = mystr & skn & vbcrlf
        Next
        mystr = mystr & "" & vbcrlf
    End If

    if                            oreg.EnumKey(HKEY_LOCAL_MACHINE,
"SOFTWARE\Wow6432Node\Microsoft\Jet 4.0\ISAM Formats", SubKeyNames) = 0
then
        mystr     =     mystr     &     "Found    Jet    4.0    ISAMS    in
HKEY_LOCAL_MACHINE\Wow6432Node\Microsoft\Jet 4.0\ISAM Formats" & vbcrlf
```

```vbscript
    mystr = mystr & "" & vbcrlf
    for each skn in SubKeyNames
        mystr = mystr & skn & vbcrlf
    Next
    mystr = mystr & "" & vbcrlf
End If


    if                              oReg.EnumKey(HKEY_LOCAL_MACHINE,
"SOFTWARE\Wow6432Node\Microsoft\Office\10.0\Access Connectivity Engine\ISAM
Formats", SubKeyNames) = 0 then
        mystr   =   mystr   &   "Found   ACE   10.0   ISAMS   in
SOFTWARE\Wow6432Node\Microsoft\Office\10.0\Access  Connectivity  Engine\ISAM
Formats" & vbcrlf
    mystr = mystr & "" & vbcrlf
    for each skn in SubKeyNames
        mystr = mystr & skn & vbcrlf
    Next
    mystr = mystr & "" & vbcrlf
End If


    if                              oReg.EnumKey(HKEY_LOCAL_MACHINE,
"SOFTWARE\Wow6432Node\Microsoft\Office\12.0\Access  Connectivity  Engine\ISAM
Formats", SubKeyNames) = 0 then
        mystr   =   mystr   &   "Found   ACE   12.0   ISAMS   in
KEY_LOCAL_MACHHINE\SOFTWARE\Wow6432Node\Microsoft\Office\12.0\Access
Connectivity Engine\ISAM Formats" & vbcrlf
    mystr = mystr & "" & vbcrlf
    for each skn in SubKeyNames
        mystr = mystr & skn & vbcrlf
    Next
    mystr = mystr & "" & vbcrlf
End If


    if                              oReg.EnumKey(HKEY_LOCAL_MACHINE,
"SOFTWARE\Wow6432Node\Microsoft\Office\14.0\Access  Connectivity  Engine\ISAM
Formats", SubKeyNames) = 0 then
        mystr   =   mystr   &   "Found   ACE   14.0   ISAMS   in
KEY_LOCAL_MACHHINE\SOFTWARE\Wow6432Node\Microsoft\Office\14.0\Access
Connectivity Engine\ISAM Formats" & vbcrlf
    mystr = mystr & "" & vbcrlf
```

```vb
    for each skn in SubKeyNames
        mystr = mystr & skn & vbcrlf
    Next
    mystr = mystr & "" & vbcrlf
End If


    if                              oReg.EnumKey(HKEY_LOCAL_MACHINE,
"SOFTWARE\Wow6432Node\Microsoft\Office\15.0\Access Connectivity Engine\ISAM
Formats", SubKeyNames) = 0 then
        mystr    =    mystr    &    "Found    ACE    15.0    ISAMS    in
KEY_LOCAL_MACHHINE\SOFTWARE\Wow6432Node\Microsoft\Office\15.0\Access
Connectivity Engine\ISAM Formats" & vbcrlf
        mystr = mystr & "" & vbcrlf
    for each skn in SubKeyNames
        mystr = mystr & skn & vbcrlf
    Next
    mystr = mystr & "" & vbcrlf
End If


    if                              oReg.EnumKey(HKEY_LOCAL_MACHINE,
"SOFTWARE\Wow6432Node\Microsoft\Office\16.0\Access Connectivity Engine\ISAM
Formats", SubKeyNames) = 0 then
        mystr    =    mystr    &    "Found    ACE    16.0    ISAMS    in
KEY_LOCAL_MACHHINE\SOFTWARE\Wow6432Node\Microsoft\Office\16.0\Access
Connectivity Engine\ISAM Formats" & vbcrlf
        mystr = mystr & "" & vbcrlf
    for each skn in SubKeyNames
        mystr = mystr & skn & vbcrlf
    Next
    mystr = mystr & "" & vbcrlf
End If

Textarea1.innerText = mystr

End Sub

Sub Create_Template()

End Sub
```

```
Sub Add_The_StyleSheet()

    Select Case StyleSheet

        Case "None"

        Case "Basic"

            txtstream.WriteLine("<style type='text/css'>")
            txtstream.WriteLine("th")
            txtstream.WriteLine("{")
            txtstream.WriteLine("   COLOR: Darkred;")
            txtstream.WriteLine("}")
            txtstream.WriteLine("td")
            txtstream.WriteLine("{")
            txtstream.WriteLine("   COLOR: navy;")
            txtstream.WriteLine("}")
            txtstream.WriteLine("</style>")

        Case "InLine"


        Case "Table"

            txtstream.WriteLine("<style type=text/css>")
            txtstream.WriteLine("#itsthetable {")
            txtstream.WriteLine(" font-family:    Georgia,    """"""Times    New
Roman"""""", Times, serif;")
            txtstream.WriteLine(" color: #036;")
            txtstream.WriteLine("}")

            txtstream.WriteLine("caption {")
            txtstream.WriteLine(" font-size: 48px;")
            txtstream.WriteLine(" color: #036;")
            txtstream.WriteLine(" font-weight: bolder;")
            txtstream.WriteLine(" font-variant: small-caps;")
            txtstream.WriteLine("}")
```

```
txtstream.WriteLine("th {")
txtstream.WriteLine(" font-size: 12px;")
txtstream.WriteLine(" color: #FFF;")
txtstream.WriteLine(" background-color: #06C;")
txtstream.WriteLine(" padding: 8px 4px;")
txtstream.WriteLine(" border-bottom: 1px solid #015ebc;")
txtstream.WriteLine("}")

txtstream.WriteLine("table {")
txtstream.WriteLine(" margin: 0;")
txtstream.WriteLine(" padding: 0;")
txtstream.WriteLine(" border-collapse: collapse;")
txtstream.WriteLine(" border: 1px solid #06C;")
txtstream.WriteLine(" width: 100%")
txtstream.WriteLine("}")

txtstream.WriteLine("#itsthetable th a:link, #itsthetable th a:visited {")
txtstream.WriteLine(" color: #FFF;")
txtstream.WriteLine(" text-decoration: none;")
txtstream.WriteLine(" border-left: 5px solid #FFF;")
txtstream.WriteLine(" padding-left: 3px;")
txtstream.WriteLine("}")

txtstream.WriteLine("th a:hover, #itsthetable th a:active {")
txtstream.WriteLine(" color: #F90;")
txtstream.WriteLine(" text-decoration: line-through;")
txtstream.WriteLine(" border-left: 5px solid #F90;")
txtstream.WriteLine(" padding-left: 3px;")
txtstream.WriteLine("}")

txtstream.WriteLine("tbody th:hover {")
txtstream.WriteLine(" background-image: url(imgs/tbody_hover.gif);")
txtstream.WriteLine(" background-position: bottom;")
txtstream.WriteLine(" background-repeat: repeat-x;")
txtstream.WriteLine("}")

txtstream.WriteLine("td {")
txtstream.WriteLine(" background-color: #f2f2f2;")
```

```
txtstream.WriteLine(" padding: 4px;")
txtstream.WriteLine(" font-size: 12px;")
txtstream.WriteLine("}")

txtstream.WriteLine("#itsthetable td:hover {")
txtstream.WriteLine(" background-color: #f8f8f8;")

txtstream.WriteLine("}")

txtstream.WriteLine("#itsthetable td a:link, #itsthetable td a:visited {")
txtstream.WriteLine(" color: #039;")
txtstream.WriteLine(" text-decoration: none;")
txtstream.WriteLine(" border-left: 3px solid #039;")
txtstream.WriteLine(" padding-left: 3px;")
txtstream.WriteLine("}")

txtstream.WriteLine("#itsthetable td a:hover, #itsthetable td a:active
{")
txtstream.WriteLine(" color: #06C;")
txtstream.WriteLine(" text-decoration: line-through;")
txtstream.WriteLine(" border-left: 3px solid #06C;")
txtstream.WriteLine(" padding-left: 3px;")
txtstream.WriteLine("}")

txtstream.WriteLine("#itsthetable th {")
txtstream.WriteLine(" text-align: left;")
txtstream.WriteLine(" width: 150px;")
txtstream.WriteLine("}")

txtstream.WriteLine("#itsthetable tr {")
txtstream.WriteLine(" border-bottom: 1px solid #CCC;")
txtstream.WriteLine("}")

txtstream.WriteLine("#itsthetable thead th {")
txtstream.WriteLine(" background-image: url(imgs/thead_back.gif);")
txtstream.WriteLine(" background-repeat: repeat-x;")
txtstream.WriteLine(" background-color: #06C;")
txtstream.WriteLine(" height: 30px;")
txtstream.WriteLine(" font-size: 18px;")
txtstream.WriteLine(" text-align: center;")
```

```
txtstream.WriteLine(" text-shadow: #333 2px 2px;")
txtstream.WriteLine(" border: 2px;")
txtstream.WriteLine("}")

txtstream.WriteLine("#itsthetable tfoot th {")
txtstream.WriteLine(" background-image: url(imgs/tfoot_back.gif);")
txtstream.WriteLine(" background-repeat: repeat-x;")
txtstream.WriteLine(" background-color: #036;")
txtstream.WriteLine(" height: 30px;")
txtstream.WriteLine(" font-size: 28px;")
txtstream.WriteLine(" text-align: center;")
txtstream.WriteLine(" text-shadow: #333 2px 2px;")
txtstream.WriteLine("}")

txtstream.WriteLine("#itsthetable tfoot td {")
txtstream.WriteLine(" background-image: url(imgs/tfoot_back.gif);")
txtstream.WriteLine(" background-repeat: repeat-x;")
txtstream.WriteLine(" background-color: #036;")
txtstream.WriteLine(" color: FFF;")
txtstream.WriteLine(" height: 30px;")
txtstream.WriteLine(" font-size: 24px;")
txtstream.WriteLine(" text-align: left;")
txtstream.WriteLine(" text-shadow: #333 2px 2px;")
txtstream.WriteLine("}")

txtstream.WriteLine("tbody td a[href="""""http://www.csslab.cl/"""""]
{")
txtstream.WriteLine(" font-weight: bolder;")
txtstream.WriteLine("}")
txtstream.WriteLine("</style>")


        Case "BlackAndWhiteText"


txtstream.WriteLine("<style type='text/css'>")
txtstream.WriteLine("th")
txtstream.WriteLine("{")
txtstream.WriteLine("   COLOR: white;")
txtstream.WriteLine("   BACKGROUND-COLOR: black;")
```

```
txtstream.WriteLine("    FONT-FAMILY:font-family: Cambria, serif;")
txtstream.WriteLine("    FONT-SIZE: 12px;")
txtstream.WriteLine("    text-align: left;")
txtstream.WriteLine("    white-Space: nowrap;")
txtstream.WriteLine("}")
txtstream.WriteLine("td")
txtstream.WriteLine("{")
txtstream.WriteLine("    COLOR: white;")
txtstream.WriteLine("    BACKGROUND-COLOR: black;")
txtstream.WriteLine("    FONT-FAMILY: font-family: Cambria, serif;")
txtstream.WriteLine("    FONT-SIZE: 12px;")
txtstream.WriteLine("    text-align: left;")
txtstream.WriteLine("    white-Space: nowrap;")
txtstream.WriteLine("}")
txtstream.WriteLine("div")
txtstream.WriteLine("{")
txtstream.WriteLine("    COLOR: white;")
txtstream.WriteLine("    BACKGROUND-COLOR: black;")
txtstream.WriteLine("    FONT-FAMILY: font-family: Cambria, serif;")
txtstream.WriteLine("    FONT-SIZE: 10px;")
txtstream.WriteLine("    text-align: left;")
txtstream.WriteLine("    white-Space: nowrap;")
txtstream.WriteLine("}")
txtstream.WriteLine("span")
txtstream.WriteLine("{")
txtstream.WriteLine("    COLOR: white;")
txtstream.WriteLine("    BACKGROUND-COLOR: black;")
txtstream.WriteLine("    FONT-FAMILY: font-family: Cambria, serif;")
txtstream.WriteLine("    FONT-SIZE: 10px;")
txtstream.WriteLine("    text-align: left;")
txtstream.WriteLine("    white-Space: nowrap;")
txtstream.WriteLine("    display:inline-block;")
txtstream.WriteLine("    width: 100%;")
txtstream.WriteLine("}")
txtstream.WriteLine("textarea")
txtstream.WriteLine("{")
txtstream.WriteLine("    COLOR: white;")
txtstream.WriteLine("    BACKGROUND-COLOR: black;")
txtstream.WriteLine("    FONT-FAMILY: font-family: Cambria, serif;")
txtstream.WriteLine("    FONT-SIZE: 10px;")
```

```
        txtstream.WriteLine("    text-align: left;")
        txtstream.WriteLine("    white-Space: nowrap;")
        txtstream.WriteLine("    width: 100%;")
        txtstream.WriteLine("}")
        txtstream.WriteLine("select")
        txtstream.WriteLine("{")
        txtstream.WriteLine("    COLOR: white;")
        txtstream.WriteLine("    BACKGROUND-COLOR: black;")
        txtstream.WriteLine("    FONT-FAMILY: font-family: Cambria, serif;")
        txtstream.WriteLine("    FONT-SIZE: 10px;")
        txtstream.WriteLine("    text-align: left;")
        txtstream.WriteLine("    white-Space: nowrap;")
        txtstream.WriteLine("    width: 100%;")
        txtstream.WriteLine("}")
        txtstream.WriteLine("input")
        txtstream.WriteLine("{")
        txtstream.WriteLine("    COLOR: white;")
        txtstream.WriteLine("    BACKGROUND-COLOR: black;")
        txtstream.WriteLine("    FONT-FAMILY: font-family: Cambria, serif;")
        txtstream.WriteLine("    FONT-SIZE: 12px;")
        txtstream.WriteLine("    text-align: left;")
        txtstream.WriteLine("    display:table-cell;")
        txtstream.WriteLine("    white-Space: nowrap;")
        txtstream.WriteLine("}")
        txtstream.WriteLine("h1 {")
        txtstream.WriteLine("color: antiquewhite;")
        txtstream.WriteLine("text-shadow: 1px 1px 1px black;")
        txtstream.WriteLine("padding: 3px;")
        txtstream.WriteLine("text-align: center;")
        txtstream.WriteLine("box-shadow: in2px 2px 5px rgba(0,0,0,0.5), in-
2px -2px 5px rgba(255,255,255,0.5);")
        txtstream.WriteLine("}")
        txtstream.WriteLine("</style>")

    Case "ColoredText"

        txtstream.WriteLine("<style type='text/css'>")
        txtstream.WriteLine("th")
        txtstream.WriteLine("{")
        txtstream.WriteLine("    COLOR: darkred;")
```

```
txtstream.WriteLine("  BACKGROUND-COLOR: #eeeeee;")
txtstream.WriteLine("  FONT-FAMILY:font-family: Cambria, serif;")
txtstream.WriteLine("  FONT-SIZE: 12px;")
txtstream.WriteLine("  text-align: left;")
txtstream.WriteLine("  white-Space: nowrap;")
txtstream.WriteLine("}")
txtstream.WriteLine("td")
txtstream.WriteLine("{")
txtstream.WriteLine("  COLOR: navy;")
txtstream.WriteLine("  BACKGROUND-COLOR: #eeeeee;")
txtstream.WriteLine("  FONT-FAMILY: font-family: Cambria, serif;")
txtstream.WriteLine("  FONT-SIZE: 12px;")
txtstream.WriteLine("  text-align: left;")
txtstream.WriteLine("  white-Space: nowrap;")
txtstream.WriteLine("}")
txtstream.WriteLine("div")
txtstream.WriteLine("{")
txtstream.WriteLine("  COLOR: white;")
txtstream.WriteLine("  BACKGROUND-COLOR: navy;")
txtstream.WriteLine("  FONT-FAMILY: font-family: Cambria, serif;")
txtstream.WriteLine("  FONT-SIZE: 10px;")
txtstream.WriteLine("  text-align: left;")
txtstream.WriteLine("  white-Space: nowrap;")
txtstream.WriteLine("}")
txtstream.WriteLine("span")
txtstream.WriteLine("{")
txtstream.WriteLine("  COLOR: white;")
txtstream.WriteLine("  BACKGROUND-COLOR: navy;")
txtstream.WriteLine("  FONT-FAMILY: font-family: Cambria, serif;")
txtstream.WriteLine("  FONT-SIZE: 10px;")
txtstream.WriteLine("  text-align: left;")
txtstream.WriteLine("  white-Space: nowrap;")
txtstream.WriteLine("  display:inline-block;")
txtstream.WriteLine("  width: 100%;")
txtstream.WriteLine("}")
txtstream.WriteLine("textarea")
txtstream.WriteLine("{")
txtstream.WriteLine("  COLOR: white;")
txtstream.WriteLine("  BACKGROUND-COLOR: navy;")
txtstream.WriteLine("  FONT-FAMILY: font-family: Cambria, serif;")
```

```
        txtstream.WriteLine("   FONT-SIZE: 10px;")
        txtstream.WriteLine("   text-align: left;")
        txtstream.WriteLine("   white-Space: nowrap;")
        txtstream.WriteLine("   width: 100%;")
        txtstream.WriteLine("}")
        txtstream.WriteLine("select")
        txtstream.WriteLine("{")
        txtstream.WriteLine("   COLOR: white;")
        txtstream.WriteLine("   BACKGROUND-COLOR: navy;")
        txtstream.WriteLine("   FONT-FAMILY: font-family: Cambria, serif;")
        txtstream.WriteLine("   FONT-SIZE: 10px;")
        txtstream.WriteLine("   text-align: left;")
        txtstream.WriteLine("   white-Space: nowrap;")
        txtstream.WriteLine("   width: 100%;")
        txtstream.WriteLine("}")
        txtstream.WriteLine("input")
        txtstream.WriteLine("{")
        txtstream.WriteLine("   COLOR: white;")
        txtstream.WriteLine("   BACKGROUND-COLOR: navy;")
        txtstream.WriteLine("   FONT-FAMILY: font-family: Cambria, serif;")
        txtstream.WriteLine("   FONT-SIZE: 12px;")
        txtstream.WriteLine("   text-align: left;")
        txtstream.WriteLine("   display:table-cell;")
        txtstream.WriteLine("   white-Space: nowrap;")
        txtstream.WriteLine("}")
        txtstream.WriteLine("h1 {")
        txtstream.WriteLine("color: antiquewhite;")
        txtstream.WriteLine("text-shadow: 1px 1px 1px black;")
        txtstream.WriteLine("padding: 3px;")
        txtstream.WriteLine("text-align: center;")
        txtstream.WriteLine("box-shadow: in2px 2px 5px rgba(0,0,0,0.5), in-
2px -2px 5px rgba(255,255,255,0.5);")
        txtstream.WriteLine("}")
        txtstream.WriteLine("</style>")


    Case "OscillatingRowColors"


        txtstream.WriteLine("<style type='text/css'> ")
```

```
txtstream.WriteLine("th")
txtstream.WriteLine("{")
txtstream.WriteLine("    COLOR: white;")
txtstream.WriteLine("    BACKGROUND-COLOR: navy;")
txtstream.WriteLine("    FONT-FAMILY:font-family: Cambria, serif;")
txtstream.WriteLine("    FONT-SIZE: 12px;")
txtstream.WriteLine("    text-align: left;")
txtstream.WriteLine("    white-Space: nowrap;")
txtstream.WriteLine("}")
txtstream.WriteLine("td")
txtstream.WriteLine("{")
txtstream.WriteLine("    COLOR: navy;")
txtstream.WriteLine("    FONT-FAMILY: font-family: Cambria, serif;")
txtstream.WriteLine("    FONT-SIZE: 12px;")
txtstream.WriteLine("    text-align: left;")
txtstream.WriteLine("    white-Space: nowrap;")
txtstream.WriteLine("}")
txtstream.WriteLine("div")
txtstream.WriteLine("{")
txtstream.WriteLine("    COLOR: navy;")
txtstream.WriteLine("    FONT-FAMILY: font-family: Cambria, serif;")
txtstream.WriteLine("    FONT-SIZE: 12px;")
txtstream.WriteLine("    text-align: left;")
txtstream.WriteLine("    white-Space: nowrap;")
txtstream.WriteLine("}")
txtstream.WriteLine("span")
txtstream.WriteLine("{")
txtstream.WriteLine("    COLOR: navy;")
txtstream.WriteLine("    FONT-FAMILY: font-family: Cambria, serif;")
txtstream.WriteLine("    FONT-SIZE: 12px;")
txtstream.WriteLine("    text-align: left;")
txtstream.WriteLine("    white-Space: nowrap;")
txtstream.WriteLine("    width: 100%;")
txtstream.WriteLine("}")
txtstream.WriteLine("textarea")
txtstream.WriteLine("{")
txtstream.WriteLine("    COLOR: navy;")
txtstream.WriteLine("    FONT-FAMILY: font-family: Cambria, serif;")
txtstream.WriteLine("    FONT-SIZE: 12px;")
txtstream.WriteLine("    text-align: left;")
```

```
txtstream.WriteLine("    white-Space: nowrap;")
txtstream.WriteLine("    display:inline-block;")
txtstream.WriteLine("    width: 100%;")
txtstream.WriteLine("}")
txtstream.WriteLine("select")
txtstream.WriteLine("{")
txtstream.WriteLine("    COLOR: navy;")
txtstream.WriteLine("    FONT-FAMILY: font-family: Cambria, serif;")
txtstream.WriteLine("    FONT-SIZE: 10px;")
txtstream.WriteLine("    text-align: left;")
txtstream.WriteLine("    white-Space: nowrap;")
txtstream.WriteLine("    display:inline-block;")
txtstream.WriteLine("    width: 100%;")
txtstream.WriteLine("}")
txtstream.WriteLine("input")
txtstream.WriteLine("{")
txtstream.WriteLine("    COLOR: navy;")
txtstream.WriteLine("    FONT-FAMILY: font-family: Cambria, serif;")
txtstream.WriteLine("    FONT-SIZE: 12px;")
txtstream.WriteLine("    text-align: left;")
txtstream.WriteLine("    display:table-cell;")
txtstream.WriteLine("    white-Space: nowrap;")
txtstream.WriteLine("}")
txtstream.WriteLine("h1 {")
txtstream.WriteLine("color: antiquewhite;")
txtstream.WriteLine("text-shadow: 1px 1px 1px black;")
txtstream.WriteLine("padding: 3px;")
txtstream.WriteLine("text-align: center;")
txtstream.WriteLine("box-shadow: in2px 2px 5px rgba(0,0,0,0.5), in-
2px -2px 5px rgba(255,255,255,0.5);")
txtstream.WriteLine("}")
txtstream.WriteLine("tr:nth-child(even){background-color:#f2f2f2;}")
txtstream.WriteLine("tr:nth-child(odd){background-color:#cccccc;
color:#f2f2f2;}")
txtstream.WriteLine("</style>")

Case "GhostDecorated"

txtstream.WriteLine("<style type='text/css'>")
txtstream.WriteLine("th")
```

```
txtstream.WriteLine("{")
txtstream.WriteLine("    COLOR: black;")
txtstream.WriteLine("    BACKGROUND-COLOR: white;")
txtstream.WriteLine("    FONT-FAMILY:font-family: Cambria, serif;")
txtstream.WriteLine("    FONT-SIZE: 12px;")
txtstream.WriteLine("    text-align: left;")
txtstream.WriteLine("    white-Space: nowrap;")
txtstream.WriteLine("}")
txtstream.WriteLine("td")
txtstream.WriteLine("{")
txtstream.WriteLine("    COLOR: black;")
txtstream.WriteLine("    BACKGROUND-COLOR: white;")
txtstream.WriteLine("    FONT-FAMILY: font-family: Cambria, serif;")
txtstream.WriteLine("    FONT-SIZE: 12px;")
txtstream.WriteLine("    text-align: left;")
txtstream.WriteLine("    white-Space: nowrap;")
txtstream.WriteLine("}")
txtstream.WriteLine("div")
txtstream.WriteLine("{")
txtstream.WriteLine("    COLOR: black;")
txtstream.WriteLine("    BACKGROUND-COLOR: white;")
txtstream.WriteLine("    FONT-FAMILY: font-family: Cambria, serif;")
txtstream.WriteLine("    FONT-SIZE: 10px;")
txtstream.WriteLine("    text-align: left;")
txtstream.WriteLine("    white-Space: nowrap;")
txtstream.WriteLine("}")
txtstream.WriteLine("span")
txtstream.WriteLine("{")
txtstream.WriteLine("    COLOR: black;")
txtstream.WriteLine("    BACKGROUND-COLOR: white;")
txtstream.WriteLine("    FONT-FAMILY: font-family: Cambria, serif;")
txtstream.WriteLine("    FONT-SIZE: 10px;")
txtstream.WriteLine("    text-align: left;")
txtstream.WriteLine("    white-Space: nowrap;")
txtstream.WriteLine("    display:inline-block;")
txtstream.WriteLine("    width: 100%;")
txtstream.WriteLine("}")
txtstream.WriteLine("textarea")
txtstream.WriteLine("{")
txtstream.WriteLine("    COLOR: black;")
```

```
txtstream.WriteLine("    BACKGROUND-COLOR: white;")
txtstream.WriteLine("    FONT-FAMILY: font-family: Cambria, serif;")
txtstream.WriteLine("    FONT-SIZE: 10px;")
txtstream.WriteLine("    text-align: left;")
txtstream.WriteLine("    white-Space: nowrap;")
txtstream.WriteLine("    width: 100%;")
txtstream.WriteLine("}")
txtstream.WriteLine("select")
txtstream.WriteLine("{")
txtstream.WriteLine("    COLOR: black;")
txtstream.WriteLine("    BACKGROUND-COLOR: white;")
txtstream.WriteLine("    FONT-FAMILY: font-family: Cambria, serif;")
txtstream.WriteLine("    FONT-SIZE: 10px;")
txtstream.WriteLine("    text-align: left;")
txtstream.WriteLine("    white-Space: nowrap;")
txtstream.WriteLine("    width: 100%;")
txtstream.WriteLine("}")
txtstream.WriteLine("input")
txtstream.WriteLine("{")
txtstream.WriteLine("    COLOR: black;")
txtstream.WriteLine("    BACKGROUND-COLOR: white;")
txtstream.WriteLine("    FONT-FAMILY: font-family: Cambria, serif;")
txtstream.WriteLine("    FONT-SIZE: 12px;")
txtstream.WriteLine("    text-align: left;")
txtstream.WriteLine("    display:table-cell;")
txtstream.WriteLine("    white-Space: nowrap;")
txtstream.WriteLine("}")
txtstream.WriteLine("h1 {")
txtstream.WriteLine("color: antiquewhite;")
txtstream.WriteLine("text-shadow: 1px 1px 1px black;")
txtstream.WriteLine("padding: 3px;")
txtstream.WriteLine("text-align: center;")
txtstream.WriteLine("box-shadow: in2px 2px 5px rgba(0,0,0,0.5), in-
2px -2px 5px rgba(255,255,255,0.5);")
txtstream.WriteLine("}")
txtstream.WriteLine("</style>")

        Case "3D"
```

```
txtstream.WriteLine("<style type='text/css'>")
txtstream.WriteLine("body")
txtstream.WriteLine("{")
txtstream.WriteLine("    PADDING-RIGHT: 0px;")
txtstream.WriteLine("    PADDING-LEFT: 0px;")
txtstream.WriteLine("    PADDING-BOTTOM: 0px;")
txtstream.WriteLine("    MARGIN: 0px;")
txtstream.WriteLine("    COLOR: #333;")
txtstream.WriteLine("    PADDING-TOP: 0px;")
txtstream.WriteLine("    FONT-FAMILY: verdana, arial, helvetica, sans-serif;")
txtstream.WriteLine("}")
txtstream.WriteLine("table")
txtstream.WriteLine("{")
txtstream.WriteLine("    BORDER-RIGHT: #999999 3px solid;")
txtstream.WriteLine("    PADDING-RIGHT: 6px;")
txtstream.WriteLine("    PADDING-LEFT: 6px;")
txtstream.WriteLine("    FONT-WEIGHT: Bold;")
txtstream.WriteLine("    FONT-SIZE: 14px;")
txtstream.WriteLine("    PADDING-BOTTOM: 6px;")
txtstream.WriteLine("    COLOR: Peru;")
txtstream.WriteLine("    LINE-HEIGHT: 14px;")
txtstream.WriteLine("    PADDING-TOP: 6px;")
txtstream.WriteLine("    BORDER-BOTTOM: #999 1px solid;")
txtstream.WriteLine("    BACKGROUND-COLOR: #eeeeee;")
txtstream.WriteLine("    FONT-FAMILY: verdana, arial, helvetica, sans-serif;")
txtstream.WriteLine("    FONT-SIZE: 12px;")
txtstream.WriteLine("}")
txtstream.WriteLine("th")
txtstream.WriteLine("{")
txtstream.WriteLine("    BORDER-RIGHT: #999999 3px solid;")
txtstream.WriteLine("    PADDING-RIGHT: 6px;")
txtstream.WriteLine("    PADDING-LEFT: 6px;")
txtstream.WriteLine("    FONT-WEIGHT: Bold;")
txtstream.WriteLine("    FONT-SIZE: 14px;")
txtstream.WriteLine("    PADDING-BOTTOM: 6px;")
txtstream.WriteLine("    COLOR: darkred;")
txtstream.WriteLine("    LINE-HEIGHT: 14px;")
txtstream.WriteLine("    PADDING-TOP: 6px;")
```

```
txtstream.WriteLine("    BORDER-BOTTOM: #999 1px solid;")
txtstream.WriteLine("    BACKGROUND-COLOR: #eeeeee;")
txtstream.WriteLine("    FONT-FAMILY:font-family: Cambria, serif;")
txtstream.WriteLine("    FONT-SIZE: 12px;")
txtstream.WriteLine("    text-align: left;")
txtstream.WriteLine("    white-Space: nowrap;")
txtstream.WriteLine("}")
txtstream.WriteLine(".th")
txtstream.WriteLine("{")
txtstream.WriteLine("    BORDER-RIGHT: #999999 2px solid;")
txtstream.WriteLine("    PADDING-RIGHT: 6px;")
txtstream.WriteLine("    PADDING-LEFT: 6px;")
txtstream.WriteLine("    FONT-WEIGHT: Bold;")
txtstream.WriteLine("    PADDING-BOTTOM: 6px;")
txtstream.WriteLine("    COLOR: black;")
txtstream.WriteLine("    PADDING-TOP: 6px;")
txtstream.WriteLine("    BORDER-BOTTOM: #999 2px solid;")
txtstream.WriteLine("    BACKGROUND-COLOR: #eeeeee;")
txtstream.WriteLine("    FONT-FAMILY: font-family: Cambria, serif;")
txtstream.WriteLine("    FONT-SIZE: 10px;")
txtstream.WriteLine("    text-align: right;")
txtstream.WriteLine("    white-Space: nowrap;")
txtstream.WriteLine("}")
txtstream.WriteLine("td")
txtstream.WriteLine("{")
txtstream.WriteLine("    BORDER-RIGHT: #999999 3px solid;")
txtstream.WriteLine("    PADDING-RIGHT: 6px;")
txtstream.WriteLine("    PADDING-LEFT: 6px;")
txtstream.WriteLine("    FONT-WEIGHT: Normal;")
txtstream.WriteLine("    PADDING-BOTTOM: 6px;")
txtstream.WriteLine("    COLOR: navy;")
txtstream.WriteLine("    LINE-HEIGHT: 14px;")
txtstream.WriteLine("    PADDING-TOP: 6px;")
txtstream.WriteLine("    BORDER-BOTTOM: #999 1px solid;")
txtstream.WriteLine("    BACKGROUND-COLOR: #eeeeee;")
txtstream.WriteLine("    FONT-FAMILY: font-family: Cambria, serif;")
txtstream.WriteLine("    FONT-SIZE: 12px;")
txtstream.WriteLine("    text-align: left;")
txtstream.WriteLine("    white-Space: nowrap;")
txtstream.WriteLine("}")
```

```
txtstream.WriteLine("div")
txtstream.WriteLine("{")
txtstream.WriteLine("    BORDER-RIGHT: #999999 3px solid;")
txtstream.WriteLine("    PADDING-RIGHT: 6px;")
txtstream.WriteLine("    PADDING-LEFT: 6px;")
txtstream.WriteLine("    FONT-WEIGHT: Normal;")
txtstream.WriteLine("    PADDING-BOTTOM: 6px;")
txtstream.WriteLine("    COLOR: white;")
txtstream.WriteLine("    PADDING-TOP: 6px;")
txtstream.WriteLine("    BORDER-BOTTOM: #999 1px solid;")
txtstream.WriteLine("    BACKGROUND-COLOR: navy;")
txtstream.WriteLine("    FONT-FAMILY: font-family: Cambria, serif;")
txtstream.WriteLine("    FONT-SIZE: 10px;")
txtstream.WriteLine("    text-align: left;")
txtstream.WriteLine("    white-Space: nowrap;")
txtstream.WriteLine("}")
txtstream.WriteLine("span")
txtstream.WriteLine("{")
txtstream.WriteLine("    BORDER-RIGHT: #999999 3px solid;")
txtstream.WriteLine("    PADDING-RIGHT: 3px;")
txtstream.WriteLine("    PADDING-LEFT: 3px;")
txtstream.WriteLine("    FONT-WEIGHT: Normal;")
txtstream.WriteLine("    PADDING-BOTTOM: 3px;")
txtstream.WriteLine("    COLOR: white;")
txtstream.WriteLine("    PADDING-TOP: 3px;")
txtstream.WriteLine("    BORDER-BOTTOM: #999 1px solid;")
txtstream.WriteLine("    BACKGROUND-COLOR: navy;")
txtstream.WriteLine("    FONT-FAMILY: font-family: Cambria, serif;")
txtstream.WriteLine("    FONT-SIZE: 10px;")
txtstream.WriteLine("    text-align: left;")
txtstream.WriteLine("    white-Space: nowrap;")
txtstream.WriteLine("    display:inline-block;")
txtstream.WriteLine("    width: 100%;")
txtstream.WriteLine("}")
txtstream.WriteLine("textarea")
txtstream.WriteLine("{")
txtstream.WriteLine("    BORDER-RIGHT: #999999 3px solid;")
txtstream.WriteLine("    PADDING-RIGHT: 3px;")
txtstream.WriteLine("    PADDING-LEFT: 3px;")
txtstream.WriteLine("    FONT-WEIGHT: Normal;")
```

```
txtstream.WriteLine("    PADDING-BOTTOM: 3px;")
txtstream.WriteLine("    COLOR: white;")
txtstream.WriteLine("    PADDING-TOP: 3px;")
txtstream.WriteLine("    BORDER-BOTTOM: #999 1px solid;")
txtstream.WriteLine("    BACKGROUND-COLOR: navy;")
txtstream.WriteLine("    FONT-FAMILY: font-family: Cambria, serif;")
txtstream.WriteLine("    FONT-SIZE: 10px;")
txtstream.WriteLine("    text-align: left;")
txtstream.WriteLine("    white-Space: nowrap;")
txtstream.WriteLine("    width: 100%;")
txtstream.WriteLine("}")
txtstream.WriteLine("select")
txtstream.WriteLine("{")
txtstream.WriteLine("    BORDER-RIGHT: #999999 3px solid;")
txtstream.WriteLine("    PADDING-RIGHT: 6px;")
txtstream.WriteLine("    PADDING-LEFT: 6px;")
txtstream.WriteLine("    FONT-WEIGHT: Normal;")
txtstream.WriteLine("    PADDING-BOTTOM: 6px;")
txtstream.WriteLine("    COLOR: white;")
txtstream.WriteLine("    PADDING-TOP: 6px;")
txtstream.WriteLine("    BORDER-BOTTOM: #999 1px solid;")
txtstream.WriteLine("    BACKGROUND-COLOR: navy;")
txtstream.WriteLine("    FONT-FAMILY: font-family: Cambria, serif;")
txtstream.WriteLine("    FONT-SIZE: 10px;")
txtstream.WriteLine("    text-align: left;")
txtstream.WriteLine("    white-Space: nowrap;")
txtstream.WriteLine("    width: 100%;")
txtstream.WriteLine("}")
txtstream.WriteLine("input")
txtstream.WriteLine("{")
txtstream.WriteLine("    BORDER-RIGHT: #999999 3px solid;")
txtstream.WriteLine("    PADDING-RIGHT: 3px;")
txtstream.WriteLine("    PADDING-LEFT: 3px;")
txtstream.WriteLine("    FONT-WEIGHT: Bold;")
txtstream.WriteLine("    PADDING-BOTTOM: 3px;")
txtstream.WriteLine("    COLOR: white;")
txtstream.WriteLine("    PADDING-TOP: 3px;")
txtstream.WriteLine("    BORDER-BOTTOM: #999 1px solid;")
txtstream.WriteLine("    BACKGROUND-COLOR: navy;")
txtstream.WriteLine("    FONT-FAMILY: font-family: Cambria, serif;")
```

```
            txtstream.WriteLine("   FONT-SIZE: 12px;")
            txtstream.WriteLine("   text-align: left;")
            txtstream.WriteLine("   display:table-cell;")
            txtstream.WriteLine("   white-Space: nowrap;")
            txtstream.WriteLine("   width: 100%;")
            txtstream.WriteLine("}")
            txtstream.WriteLine("h1 {")
            txtstream.WriteLine("color: antiquewhite;")
            txtstream.WriteLine("text-shadow: 1px 1px 1px black;")
            txtstream.WriteLine("padding: 3px;")
            txtstream.WriteLine("text-align: center;")
            txtstream.WriteLine("box-shadow: in2px 2px 5px rgba(0,0,0,0.5), in-
2px -2px 5px rgba(255,255,255,0.5);")
            txtstream.WriteLine("}")
            txtstream.WriteLine("</style>")

        Case "ShadowBox"

            txtstream.WriteLine("<style type='text/css'>")
            txtstream.WriteLine("body")
            txtstream.WriteLine("{")
            txtstream.WriteLine("   PADDING-RIGHT: 0px;")
            txtstream.WriteLine("   PADDING-LEFT: 0px;")
            txtstream.WriteLine("   PADDING-BOTTOM: 0px;")
            txtstream.WriteLine("   MARGIN: 0px;")
            txtstream.WriteLine("   COLOR: #333;")
            txtstream.WriteLine("   PADDING-TOP: 0px;")
            txtstream.WriteLine("   FONT-FAMILY: verdana, arial, helvetica, sans-
serif;")
            txtstream.WriteLine("}")
            txtstream.WriteLine("table")
            txtstream.WriteLine("{")
            txtstream.WriteLine("   BORDER-RIGHT: #999999 1px solid;")
            txtstream.WriteLine("   PADDING-RIGHT: 1px;")
            txtstream.WriteLine("   PADDING-LEFT: 1px;")
            txtstream.WriteLine("   PADDING-BOTTOM: 1px;")
            txtstream.WriteLine("   LINE-HEIGHT: 8px;")
            txtstream.WriteLine("   PADDING-TOP: 1px;")
            txtstream.WriteLine("   BORDER-BOTTOM: #999 1px solid;")
            txtstream.WriteLine("   BACKGROUND-COLOR: #eeeeee;")
```

```
            txtstream.WriteLine("
filter:progid:DXImageTransform.Microsoft.Shadow(color='silver',        Direction=135,
Strength=16)")
            txtstream.WriteLine("}")
            txtstream.WriteLine("th")
            txtstream.WriteLine("{")
            txtstream.WriteLine("  BORDER-RIGHT: #999999 3px solid;")
            txtstream.WriteLine("  PADDING-RIGHT: 6px;")
            txtstream.WriteLine("  PADDING-LEFT: 6px;")
            txtstream.WriteLine("  FONT-WEIGHT: Bold;")
            txtstream.WriteLine("  FONT-SIZE: 14px;")
            txtstream.WriteLine("  PADDING-BOTTOM: 6px;")
            txtstream.WriteLine("  COLOR: darkred;")
            txtstream.WriteLine("  LINE-HEIGHT: 14px;")
            txtstream.WriteLine("  PADDING-TOP: 6px;")
            txtstream.WriteLine("  BORDER-BOTTOM: #999 1px solid;")
            txtstream.WriteLine("  BACKGROUND-COLOR: #eeeeee;")
            txtstream.WriteLine("  FONT-FAMILY: font-family: Cambria, serif;")
            txtstream.WriteLine("  FONT-SIZE: 12px;")
            txtstream.WriteLine("  text-align: left;")
            txtstream.WriteLine("  white-Space: nowrap;")
            txtstream.WriteLine("}")
            txtstream.WriteLine(".th")
            txtstream.WriteLine("{")
            txtstream.WriteLine("  BORDER-RIGHT: #999999 2px solid;")
            txtstream.WriteLine("  PADDING-RIGHT: 6px;")
            txtstream.WriteLine("  PADDING-LEFT: 6px;")
            txtstream.WriteLine("  FONT-WEIGHT: Bold;")
            txtstream.WriteLine("  PADDING-BOTTOM: 6px;")
            txtstream.WriteLine("  COLOR: black;")
            txtstream.WriteLine("  PADDING-TOP: 6px;")
            txtstream.WriteLine("  BORDER-BOTTOM: #999 2px solid;")
            txtstream.WriteLine("  BACKGROUND-COLOR: #eeeeee;")
            txtstream.WriteLine("  FONT-FAMILY: font-family: Cambria, serif;")
            txtstream.WriteLine("  FONT-SIZE: 10px;")
            txtstream.WriteLine("  text-align: right;")
            txtstream.WriteLine("  white-Space: nowrap;")
            txtstream.WriteLine("}")
            txtstream.WriteLine("td")
            txtstream.WriteLine("{")
```

```
txtstream.WriteLine("    BORDER-RIGHT: #999999 3px solid;")
txtstream.WriteLine("    PADDING-RIGHT: 6px;")
txtstream.WriteLine("    PADDING-LEFT: 6px;")
txtstream.WriteLine("    FONT-WEIGHT: Normal;")
txtstream.WriteLine("    PADDING-BOTTOM: 6px;")
txtstream.WriteLine("    COLOR: navy;")
txtstream.WriteLine("    LINE-HEIGHT: 14px;")
txtstream.WriteLine("    PADDING-TOP: 6px;")
txtstream.WriteLine("    BORDER-BOTTOM: #999 1px solid;")
txtstream.WriteLine("    BACKGROUND-COLOR: #eeeeee;")
txtstream.WriteLine("    FONT-FAMILY: font-family: Cambria, serif;")
txtstream.WriteLine("    FONT-SIZE: 12px;")
txtstream.WriteLine("    text-align: left;")
txtstream.WriteLine("    white-Space: nowrap;")
txtstream.WriteLine("}")
txtstream.WriteLine("div")
txtstream.WriteLine("{")
txtstream.WriteLine("    BORDER-RIGHT: #999999 3px solid;")
txtstream.WriteLine("    PADDING-RIGHT: 6px;")
txtstream.WriteLine("    PADDING-LEFT: 6px;")
txtstream.WriteLine("    FONT-WEIGHT: Normal;")
txtstream.WriteLine("    PADDING-BOTTOM: 6px;")
txtstream.WriteLine("    COLOR: white;")
txtstream.WriteLine("    PADDING-TOP: 6px;")
txtstream.WriteLine("    BORDER-BOTTOM: #999 1px solid;")
txtstream.WriteLine("    BACKGROUND-COLOR: navy;")
txtstream.WriteLine("    FONT-FAMILY: font-family: Cambria, serif;")
txtstream.WriteLine("    FONT-SIZE: 10px;")
txtstream.WriteLine("    text-align: left;")
txtstream.WriteLine("    white-Space: nowrap;")
txtstream.WriteLine("}")
txtstream.WriteLine("span")
txtstream.WriteLine("{")
txtstream.WriteLine("    BORDER-RIGHT: #999999 3px solid;")
txtstream.WriteLine("    PADDING-RIGHT: 3px;")
txtstream.WriteLine("    PADDING-LEFT: 3px;")
txtstream.WriteLine("    FONT-WEIGHT: Normal;")
txtstream.WriteLine("    PADDING-BOTTOM: 3px;")
txtstream.WriteLine("    COLOR: white;")
txtstream.WriteLine("    PADDING-TOP: 3px;")
```

```
txtstream.WriteLine("    BORDER-BOTTOM: #999 1px solid;")
txtstream.WriteLine("    BACKGROUND-COLOR: navy;")
txtstream.WriteLine("    FONT-FAMILY: font-family: Cambria, serif;")
txtstream.WriteLine("    FONT-SIZE: 10px;")
txtstream.WriteLine("    text-align: left;")
txtstream.WriteLine("    white-Space: nowrap;")
txtstream.WriteLine("    display: inline-block;")
txtstream.WriteLine("    width: 100%;")
txtstream.WriteLine("}")
txtstream.WriteLine("textarea")
txtstream.WriteLine("{")
txtstream.WriteLine("    BORDER-RIGHT: #999999 3px solid;")
txtstream.WriteLine("    PADDING-RIGHT: 3px;")
txtstream.WriteLine("    PADDING-LEFT: 3px;")
txtstream.WriteLine("    FONT-WEIGHT: Normal;")
txtstream.WriteLine("    PADDING-BOTTOM: 3px;")
txtstream.WriteLine("    COLOR: white;")
txtstream.WriteLine("    PADDING-TOP: 3px;")
txtstream.WriteLine("    BORDER-BOTTOM: #999 1px solid;")
txtstream.WriteLine("    BACKGROUND-COLOR: navy;")
txtstream.WriteLine("    FONT-FAMILY: font-family: Cambria, serif;")
txtstream.WriteLine("    FONT-SIZE: 10px;")
txtstream.WriteLine("    text-align: left;")
txtstream.WriteLine("    white-Space: nowrap;")
txtstream.WriteLine("    width: 100%;")
txtstream.WriteLine("}")
txtstream.WriteLine("select")
txtstream.WriteLine("{")
txtstream.WriteLine("    BORDER-RIGHT: #999999 3px solid;")
txtstream.WriteLine("    PADDING-RIGHT: 6px;")
txtstream.WriteLine("    PADDING-LEFT: 6px;")
txtstream.WriteLine("    FONT-WEIGHT: Normal;")
txtstream.WriteLine("    PADDING-BOTTOM: 6px;")
txtstream.WriteLine("    COLOR: white;")
txtstream.WriteLine("    PADDING-TOP: 6px;")
txtstream.WriteLine("    BORDER-BOTTOM: #999 1px solid;")
txtstream.WriteLine("    BACKGROUND-COLOR: navy;")
txtstream.WriteLine("    FONT-FAMILY: font-family: Cambria, serif;")
txtstream.WriteLine("    FONT-SIZE: 10px;")
txtstream.WriteLine("    text-align: left;")
```

```
txtstream.WriteLine("    white-Space: nowrap;")
txtstream.WriteLine("    width: 100%;")
txtstream.WriteLine("}")
txtstream.WriteLine("input")
txtstream.WriteLine("{")
txtstream.WriteLine("    BORDER-RIGHT: #999999 3px solid;")
txtstream.WriteLine("    PADDING-RIGHT: 3px;")
txtstream.WriteLine("    PADDING-LEFT: 3px;")
txtstream.WriteLine("    FONT-WEIGHT: Bold;")
txtstream.WriteLine("    PADDING-BOTTOM: 3px;")
txtstream.WriteLine("    COLOR: white;")
txtstream.WriteLine("    PADDING-TOP: 3px;")
txtstream.WriteLine("    BORDER-BOTTOM: #999 1px solid;")
txtstream.WriteLine("    BACKGROUND-COLOR: navy;")
txtstream.WriteLine("    FONT-FAMILY: font-family: Cambria, serif;")
txtstream.WriteLine("    FONT-SIZE: 12px;")
txtstream.WriteLine("    text-align: left;")
txtstream.WriteLine("    display: table-cell;")
txtstream.WriteLine("    white-Space: nowrap;")
txtstream.WriteLine("    width: 100%;")
txtstream.WriteLine("}")
txtstream.WriteLine("h1 {")
txtstream.WriteLine("color: antiquewhite;")
txtstream.WriteLine("text-shadow: 1px 1px 1px black;")
txtstream.WriteLine("padding: 3px;")
txtstream.WriteLine("text-align: center;")
txtstream.WriteLine("box-shadow: in2px 2px 5px rgba(0,0,0,0.5), in-2px -2px 5px rgba(255,255,255,0.5);")
txtstream.WriteLine("}")
txtstream.WriteLine("</style>")

        Case "Customized"

txtstream.WriteLine("<style type='text/css'>")
txtstream.WriteLine("body")
txtstream.WriteLine("{")
txtstream.WriteLine("    PADDING-RIGHT: 0px;")
txtstream.WriteLine("    PADDING-LEFT: 0px;")
txtstream.WriteLine("    PADDING-BOTTOM: 0px;")
txtstream.WriteLine("    MARGIN: 0px;")
```

```
txtstream.WriteLine("    COLOR: #333;")
txtstream.WriteLine("    PADDING-TOP: 0px;")
txtstream.WriteLine("    FONT-FAMILY: verdana, arial, helvetica, sans-serif;")
txtstream.WriteLine("}")
txtstream.WriteLine("Table")
txtstream.WriteLine("{")
txtstream.WriteLine("    BORDER-RIGHT: #999999 1px solid;")
txtstream.WriteLine("    PADDING-RIGHT: 1px;")
txtstream.WriteLine("    PADDING-LEFT: 1px;")
txtstream.WriteLine("    PADDING-BOTTOM: 1px;")
txtstream.WriteLine("    LINE-HEIGHT: 8px;")
txtstream.WriteLine("    PADDING-TOP: 1px;")
txtstream.WriteLine("    BORDER-BOTTOM: #999 1px solid;")
txtstream.WriteLine("    BACKGROUND-COLOR: #eeeeee;")
txtstream.WriteLine("    filter:progid:DXImageTransform.Microsoft.Shadow(color='silver',    Direction=135, Strength=16)")
txtstream.WriteLine("}")
txtstream.WriteLine("th")
txtstream.WriteLine("{")
txtstream.WriteLine("    BORDER-RIGHT: #999999 3px solid;")
txtstream.WriteLine("    PADDING-RIGHT: 6px;")
txtstream.WriteLine("    PADDING-LEFT: 6px;")
txtstream.WriteLine("    FONT-WEIGHT: Bold;")
txtstream.WriteLine("    FONT-SIZE: 14px;")
txtstream.WriteLine("    PADDING-BOTTOM: 6px;")
txtstream.WriteLine("    COLOR: darkred;")
txtstream.WriteLine("    LINE-HEIGHT: 14px;")
txtstream.WriteLine("    PADDING-TOP: 6px;")
txtstream.WriteLine("    BORDER-BOTTOM: #999 1px solid;")
txtstream.WriteLine("    BACKGROUND-COLOR: #eeeeee;")
txtstream.WriteLine("    FONT-FAMILY: font-family: Cambria, serif;")
txtstream.WriteLine("    FONT-SIZE: 12px;")
txtstream.WriteLine("    text-align: left;")
txtstream.WriteLine("    white-Space: nowrap;")
txtstream.WriteLine("}")
txtstream.WriteLine(".th")
txtstream.WriteLine("{")
txtstream.WriteLine("    BORDER-RIGHT: #999999 2px solid;")
```

```
txtstream.WriteLine("    PADDING-RIGHT: 6px;")
txtstream.WriteLine("    PADDING-LEFT: 6px;")
txtstream.WriteLine("    FONT-WEIGHT: Bold;")
txtstream.WriteLine("    PADDING-BOTTOM: 6px;")
txtstream.WriteLine("    COLOR: black;")
txtstream.WriteLine("    PADDING-TOP: 6px;")
txtstream.WriteLine("    BORDER-BOTTOM: #999 2px solid;")
txtstream.WriteLine("    BACKGROUND-COLOR: #eeeeee;")
txtstream.WriteLine("    FONT-FAMILY: font-family: Cambria, serif;")
txtstream.WriteLine("    FONT-SIZE: 10px;")
txtstream.WriteLine("    text-align: right;")
txtstream.WriteLine("    white-Space: nowrap;")
txtstream.WriteLine("}")
txtstream.WriteLine("td")
txtstream.WriteLine("{")
txtstream.WriteLine("    BORDER-RIGHT: #999999 3px solid;")
txtstream.WriteLine("    PADDING-RIGHT: 6px;")
txtstream.WriteLine("    PADDING-LEFT: 6px;")
txtstream.WriteLine("    FONT-WEIGHT: Normal;")
txtstream.WriteLine("    PADDING-BOTTOM: 6px;")
txtstream.WriteLine("    COLOR: navy;")
txtstream.WriteLine("    LINE-HEIGHT: 14px;")
txtstream.WriteLine("    PADDING-TOP: 6px;")
txtstream.WriteLine("    BORDER-BOTTOM: #999 1px solid;")
txtstream.WriteLine("    BACKGROUND-COLOR: #eeeeee;")
txtstream.WriteLine("    FONT-FAMILY: font-family: Cambria, serif;")
txtstream.WriteLine("    FONT-SIZE: 12px;")
txtstream.WriteLine("    text-align: left;")
txtstream.WriteLine("    white-Space: nowrap;")
txtstream.WriteLine("}")
txtstream.WriteLine("div")
txtstream.WriteLine("{")
txtstream.WriteLine("    BORDER-RIGHT: #999999 3px solid;")
txtstream.WriteLine("    PADDING-RIGHT: 6px;")
txtstream.WriteLine("    PADDING-LEFT: 6px;")
txtstream.WriteLine("    FONT-WEIGHT: Normal;")
txtstream.WriteLine("    PADDING-BOTTOM: 6px;")
txtstream.WriteLine("    COLOR: white;")
txtstream.WriteLine("    PADDING-TOP: 6px;")
txtstream.WriteLine("    BORDER-BOTTOM: #999 1px solid;")
```

```
txtstream.WriteLine("   BACKGROUND-COLOR: navy;")
txtstream.WriteLine("   FONT-FAMILY: font-family: Cambria, serif;")
txtstream.WriteLine("   FONT-SIZE: 10px;")
txtstream.WriteLine("   text-align: left;")
txtstream.WriteLine("   white-Space: nowrap;")
txtstream.WriteLine("}")
txtstream.WriteLine("span")
txtstream.WriteLine("{")
txtstream.WriteLine("   BORDER-RIGHT: #999999 3px solid;")
txtstream.WriteLine("   PADDING-RIGHT: 3px;")
txtstream.WriteLine("   PADDING-LEFT: 3px;")
txtstream.WriteLine("   FONT-WEIGHT: Normal;")
txtstream.WriteLine("   PADDING-BOTTOM: 3px;")
txtstream.WriteLine("   COLOR: white;")
txtstream.WriteLine("   PADDING-TOP: 3px;")
txtstream.WriteLine("   BORDER-BOTTOM: #999 1px solid;")
txtstream.WriteLine("   BACKGROUND-COLOR: navy;")
txtstream.WriteLine("   FONT-FAMILY: font-family: Cambria, serif;")
txtstream.WriteLine("   FONT-SIZE: 10px;")
txtstream.WriteLine("   text-align: left;")
txtstream.WriteLine("   white-Space: nowrap;")
txtstream.WriteLine("   display: inline-block;")
txtstream.WriteLine("   width: 100%;")
txtstream.WriteLine("}")
txtstream.WriteLine("textarea")
txtstream.WriteLine("{")
txtstream.WriteLine("   BORDER-RIGHT: #999999 3px solid;")
txtstream.WriteLine("   PADDING-RIGHT: 3px;")
txtstream.WriteLine("   PADDING-LEFT: 3px;")
txtstream.WriteLine("   FONT-WEIGHT: Normal;")
txtstream.WriteLine("   PADDING-BOTTOM: 3px;")
txtstream.WriteLine("   COLOR: white;")
txtstream.WriteLine("   PADDING-TOP: 3px;")
txtstream.WriteLine("   BORDER-BOTTOM: #999 1px solid;")
txtstream.WriteLine("   BACKGROUND-COLOR: navy;")
txtstream.WriteLine("   FONT-FAMILY: font-family: Cambria, serif;")
txtstream.WriteLine("   FONT-SIZE: 12px;")
txtstream.WriteLine("   text-align: left;")
txtstream.WriteLine("   width: 100%;")
txtstream.WriteLine("}")
```

```
txtstream.WriteLine("select")
txtstream.WriteLine("{")
txtstream.WriteLine("    BORDER-RIGHT: #999999 1px solid;")
txtstream.WriteLine("    PADDING-RIGHT: 1px;")
txtstream.WriteLine("    PADDING-LEFT: 1px;")
txtstream.WriteLine("    FONT-WEIGHT: Normal;")
txtstream.WriteLine("    PADDING-BOTTOM: 1px;")
txtstream.WriteLine("    COLOR: white;")
txtstream.WriteLine("    PADDING-TOP: 1px;")
txtstream.WriteLine("    BORDER-BOTTOM: #999 1px solid;")
txtstream.WriteLine("    BACKGROUND-COLOR: navy;")
txtstream.WriteLine("    FONT-FAMILY: Cambria, serif;")
txtstream.WriteLine("    FONT-SIZE: 12px;")
txtstream.WriteLine("    text-align: left;")
txtstream.WriteLine("    white-Space: nowrap;")
txtstream.WriteLine("    width: 450px;")
txtstream.WriteLine("}")
txtstream.WriteLine("select1")
txtstream.WriteLine("{")
txtstream.WriteLine("    BORDER-RIGHT: #999999 1px solid;")
txtstream.WriteLine("    PADDING-RIGHT: 1px;")
txtstream.WriteLine("    PADDING-LEFT: 1px;")
txtstream.WriteLine("    FONT-WEIGHT: Normal;")
txtstream.WriteLine("    PADDING-BOTTOM: 1px;")
txtstream.WriteLine("    COLOR: white;")
txtstream.WriteLine("    PADDING-TOP: 1px;")
txtstream.WriteLine("    BORDER-BOTTOM: #999 1px solid;")
txtstream.WriteLine("    BACKGROUND-COLOR: navy;")
txtstream.WriteLine("    FONT-FAMILY: Cambria, serif;")
txtstream.WriteLine("    FONT-SIZE: 12px;")
txtstream.WriteLine("    text-align: left;")
txtstream.WriteLine("    white-Space: nowrap;")
txtstream.WriteLine("    width: 450px;")
txtstream.WriteLine("}")
txtstream.WriteLine("select2")
txtstream.WriteLine("{")
txtstream.WriteLine("    BORDER-RIGHT: #999999 1px solid;")
txtstream.WriteLine("    PADDING-RIGHT: 1px;")
txtstream.WriteLine("    PADDING-LEFT: 1px;")
txtstream.WriteLine("    FONT-WEIGHT: Normal;")
```

```
txtstream.WriteLine("    PADDING-BOTTOM: 1px;")
txtstream.WriteLine("    COLOR: white;")
txtstream.WriteLine("    PADDING-TOP: 1px;")
txtstream.WriteLine("    BORDER-BOTTOM: #999 1px solid;")
txtstream.WriteLine("    BACKGROUND-COLOR: navy;")
txtstream.WriteLine("    FONT-FAMILY: Cambria, serif;")
txtstream.WriteLine("    FONT-SIZE: 12px;")
txtstream.WriteLine("    text-align: left;")
txtstream.WriteLine("    white-Space: nowrap;")
txtstream.WriteLine("    width: 450px;")
txtstream.WriteLine("}")
txtstream.WriteLine("select3")
txtstream.WriteLine("{")
txtstream.WriteLine("    BORDER-RIGHT: #999999 1px solid;")
txtstream.WriteLine("    PADDING-RIGHT: 1px;")
txtstream.WriteLine("    PADDING-LEFT: 1px;")
txtstream.WriteLine("    FONT-WEIGHT: Normal;")
txtstream.WriteLine("    PADDING-BOTTOM: 1px;")
txtstream.WriteLine("    COLOR: white;")
txtstream.WriteLine("    PADDING-TOP: 1px;")
txtstream.WriteLine("    BORDER-BOTTOM: #999 1px solid;")
txtstream.WriteLine("    BACKGROUND-COLOR: navy;")
txtstream.WriteLine("    FONT-FAMILY: Cambria, serif;")
txtstream.WriteLine("    FONT-SIZE: 12px;")
txtstream.WriteLine("    text-align: left;")
txtstream.WriteLine("    white-Space: nowrap;")
txtstream.WriteLine("    width: 100px;")
txtstream.WriteLine("}")
txtstream.WriteLine("select4")
txtstream.WriteLine("{")
txtstream.WriteLine("    BORDER-RIGHT: #999999 1px solid;")
txtstream.WriteLine("    PADDING-RIGHT: 1px;")
txtstream.WriteLine("    PADDING-LEFT: 1px;")
txtstream.WriteLine("    FONT-WEIGHT: Normal;")
txtstream.WriteLine("    PADDING-BOTTOM: 1px;")
txtstream.WriteLine("    COLOR: white;")
txtstream.WriteLine("    PADDING-TOP: 1px;")
txtstream.WriteLine("    BORDER-BOTTOM: #999 1px solid;")
txtstream.WriteLine("    BACKGROUND-COLOR: navy;")
txtstream.WriteLine("    FONT-FAMILY: Cambria, serif;")
```

```
txtstream.WriteLine("    FONT-SIZE: 12px;")
txtstream.WriteLine("    text-align: left;")
txtstream.WriteLine("    white-Space: nowrap;")
txtstream.WriteLine("    width: 254px;")
txtstream.WriteLine("}")
txtstream.WriteLine("input")
txtstream.WriteLine("{")
txtstream.WriteLine("    BORDER-RIGHT: #999999 3px solid;")
txtstream.WriteLine("    PADDING-RIGHT: 3px;")
txtstream.WriteLine("    PADDING-LEFT: 3px;")
txtstream.WriteLine("    FONT-WEIGHT: Bold;")
txtstream.WriteLine("    PADDING-BOTTOM: 3px;")
txtstream.WriteLine("    COLOR: white;")
txtstream.WriteLine("    PADDING-TOP: 3px;")
txtstream.WriteLine("    BORDER-BOTTOM: #999 1px solid;")
txtstream.WriteLine("    BACKGROUND-COLOR: navy;")
txtstream.WriteLine("    FONT-FAMILY: font-family: Cambria, serif;")
txtstream.WriteLine("    FONT-SIZE: 12px;")
txtstream.WriteLine("    text-align: left;")
txtstream.WriteLine("    display: table-cell;")
txtstream.WriteLine("    white-Space: nowrap;")
txtstream.WriteLine("    width: 100%;")
txtstream.WriteLine("}")
txtstream.WriteLine("</style>")

    End Select

End Sub

</script>

</body>
</html>
```

Above this line is where it ends.

Merry Christmas!